Other titles by Ian Falloon

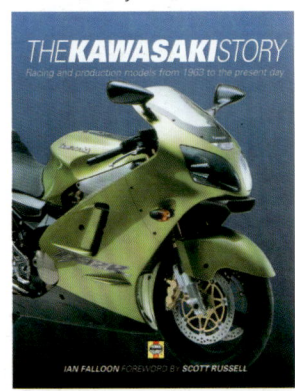
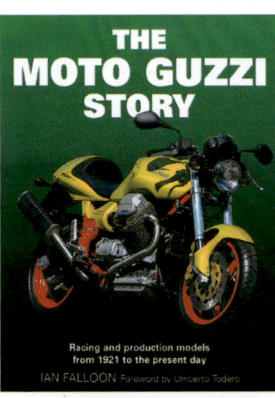
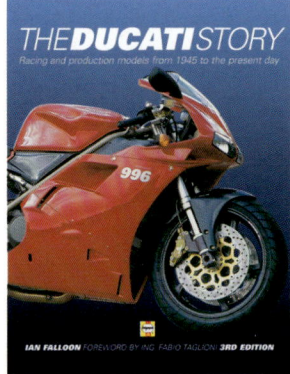
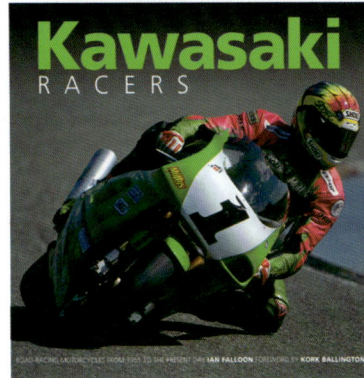
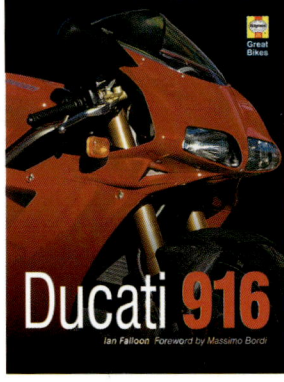
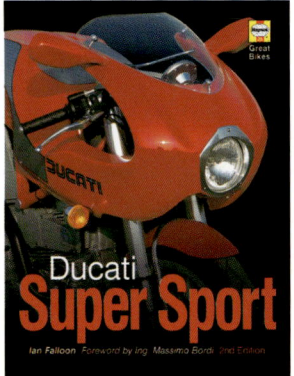

Ducati
RACERS

RACING MODELS FROM 1950 TO THE PRESENT DAY IAN FALLOON FOREWORD BY PAUL SMART

© Ian Falloon 2002

All rights reserved. No part of this publication may be reproduced, stored in a retrieval system or transmitted, in any form or by any means, electronic, mechanical, photocopying, recording or otherwise, without prior permission in writing from the publisher.

First published in 2002

A catalogue record for this book is available from the British Library

ISBN 1 85960 832 9

Library of Congress catalog card no. 2002103363

Published by Haynes Publishing, Sparkford,
Yeovil, Somerset BA22 7JJ, England

Tel: 01963 442030 Fax: 01963 440001
Int. tel: +44 1963 442030 Int. fax: +44 1963 440001
E-mail: sales@haynes-manuals.co.uk
Website: www.haynes.co.uk

Haynes North America, Inc.,
861 Lawrence Drive, Newbury Park,
California 91320, USA

Printed and bound in England by J. H. Haynes & Co Ltd, Sparkford

CONTENTS

FOREWORD BY PAUL SMART — Page **7**
INTRODUCTION AND ACKNOWLEDGEMENTS — Page **9**

1 THE MARIANNA AND BIALBERO
Page **10**

2 DESMODROMICS
Page **22**

3 CATALOGUE RACERS
Page **40**

4 PIVOTAL SUCCESS: IMOLA AND DAYTONA
Page **52**

5 THE NCR ERA: ENDURANCE AND FORMULA ONE
Page **78**

6 RACING PANTAHS
Page **96**

7 NEW GENERATION
Page **112**

8 THE 916 AND BEYOND
Page **134**

FOREWORD BY
PAUL SMART

Paul Smart setting off for the start of the most important race of his career, the 1972 Imola 200 on the desmodromic 750. *(Giovanni Perrone)*

When my wife Maggie accepted Ducati's offer of a ride on one of their new Desmo 750s in the Imola 200 in 1972, I really didn't know what to expect. I only knew of Ducatis as the singles I had once raced for Vic Camp back in the 1960s, so I doubted their 750 would be competitive as I flew into Bologna a few days before the race. After all, it would be up against the Triumphs, Kawasakis, Hondas, and Suzukis, as well as Agostini on the MV. But seeing Ing. Fabio Taglioni and his team at work immediately changed my perception and I learned that Ducati can never be underestimated. And that is the story of Ducati that continues through to this day. They may be a small company but they are prepared to take on the rest of the world and beat them. There is a compulsive passion and commitment to racing.

At the time Imola was just another victory but now it is hailed as my greatest. That also says much for Ducati. Unlike other companies they do not forget, and their history is inextricably linked to the present. From the first 125 desmos to the latest Desmoquattro Superbikes there is a clear bloodline. I am honoured to have participated in one of Ducati's greatest triumphs and it is a pleasure to be able to write the foreword to Ian Falloon's thorough and fascinating analysis of their great racing history.

Spring 2002

INTRODUCTION
AND ACKNOWLEDGEMENTS

Troy Bayliss became Ducati's fifth World Superbike champion with his victory in the 2001 championship. He started the 2002 season in scintillating fashion by winning six races in succession.
(Ian Falloon)

More than almost any other make of motorcycle, the history of Ducati is also their racing history. For more than 40 years one man, Ing. Fabio Taglioni, was responsible for virtually every significant design. Taglioni was primarily interested in racing, and even after he retired his racing legacy continued. Ducati has always been a small company in world terms, but they have achieved amazing racing success.

Ducati's racing history divides into periods involving a particular engine design. Starting with the Marianna, it moved to the desmodromic single, bevel-drive twin, Pantah, and Desmoquattro. There were anomalies and hiatuses along the way, but the history of Ducati racing is essentially the history of these five designs and their progeny. The greatest designs always won on their racing debut too: the Marianna, Desmo 125, 750 Imola, TT2, 851, and 916. With this in mind I have endeavoured to provide a new insight into the history of racing Ducatis. A conscious decision was made to concentrate on factory machinery, and those privately prepared machines that had significant victories. As well as analysing the political events that contributed to decisions, here is a 'nuts and bolts' description of racing Ducatis emphasising technicalities. It is the machinery that is important here, not just the personalities. I also treat engineers and tuners with equal importance to the riders. Race victories require riders, but riders also need competitive motorcycles. Riders often don't show an allegiance to anyone except themselves when it comes to winning, but technicians generally stay with a company for a lifetime.

When it came to discussing the machinery in detail several of the most important Ducati technicians were extremely forthcoming. Ing. Fabio Taglioni discussed his racing bikes in passionate detail on several occasions, and Steve Wynne finally provided the real story of Mike Hailwood's Isle of Man 900 NCR. Phil Schilling, creator of the California Hot-Rod, shared his intimate knowledge of early racing singles and twins, and Jonathan White, one of the bevel-drive singles' and twins' leading exponents, contributed much information on the machines of the 1960s and 1970s. Gianluigi Mengoli and Massimo Bordi recounted the birth of the more modern Pantah and Desmoquattro. Without these authoritative insights this book wouldn't be what it is and my thanks go to you all.

Over the years I have been fortunate to discuss racing Ducatis with a number of important racers and tuners. These included Rino Caracchi, Franco Farnè, Ken Kavanagh, Reno Leoni, Cook Neilson, Giuliano Pedretti, Paul Ritter, Paul Smart, and Bruno Spaggiari. Considerable assistance was provided by Museo Ducati and Ducati Corse. Livio Lodi of Museo Ducati was most enthusiastic and found a wide range of previously unpublished photos. Always supportive were Julian Thomas and Corrado Ceccinelli of Ducati Corse.

Finding suitable photographic material is as much of a challenge as writing the text, and here Mick Woollett was able to supply important colour racing photos from 1958 through until 1982. Roy Kidney and Phil Aynsley contributed many superb images, and Brian Catterson of *Cycle World*, and Ken Wootton, editor of *Australian Motorcycle News*, allowed access to their photographic archives. Others that helped were Gerolamo Bettoni, Jeremy Bowdler, Walter Breveglieri, Jerry Dean, Brian Dietz, Fred Fitzgerald, Ivar de Gier, Carlo Perelli, and Giovanni Perrone.

I would particularly like to thank my good friend Paul Smart for agreeing to write the foreword to this book. Paul is one of the pivotal riders in the history of Ducati, and one of the best ambassadors ever for the company. Thanks must also go to the late Fabio Taglioni and his wife Narina who always entertained my wife and I so lavishly, and made us feel so welcome in their house. Without Fabio Taglioni there would be no racing Ducati, so we all owe him a debt of gratitude.

Without the support of my family this book would not have eventuated. Thanks go, as always, to my wife Miriam, and sons Benjamin and Timothy.

Ian Falloon
January 2002

1 THE MARIANNA AND BIALBERO

Almost immediately after the 1955 Motogiro, Taglioni produced a 125cc version of the Marianna. On this, Giuliano Maoggi won the 1956 Motogiro outright. *(Ian Falloon)*

Although motorcycles based on the Cucciolo clip-on engine were raced from 1947, the real racing story of Ducati began with the release of the Gran Sport of 1955. Prior to the Gran Sport, Ducati's racing was confined primarily to Italy, and it was only Tamarozzi's speed records of 1950 and 1951 that provided the company with any international recognition. The Cucciolo had its limitations for competition but with the release of the 60 Sport in 1950 Ducati hoped for success in the resurrected Milano–Taranto and Motogiro d'Italia, the Gran Fondo road races. However, despite its overhead valve cylinder head, this engine was still ostensibly derived from the T3 Cucciolo. Even when enlarged to 98cc it was outclassed.

The Motogiro d'Italia was for motorcycles of less than 175cc and was held over nine days in stages held on normal Italian roads. In the first Motogiro of 1953 the 48cc Cucciolos had some success in their class, but the following year Alberto Gandossi (on the 98ohv) won two stages but could only manage third in the 100cc class. In the non-stop Milano–Taranto road race for machines up to 500cc results were even more dismal. As success in the Motogiro and Milano–Taranto was considered pivotal for sales success in Italy in the 1950s, Ducati's managing director, Dott. Giuseppe Montano, took the brave step of hiring Fabio Taglioni to design a completely new motorcycle. In a final interview with the author Taglioni said, 'Montano was so disappointed by the results in the Motogiro that he signed me on a one-year contract to design a race-winner for 1955.' Only one month after the 1954 Motogiro, Taglioni began work on the Gran Sport. Ducati's illustrious competition chronicle was underway.

Left: Franco Petrucci with the Cucciolo he rode to third in the under-75cc class in the 1951 Milano–Taranto road race. *(Museo Ducati)*

Right: The factory Cucciolo team at the ISDT held at the Valli Bergamasche in Italy in 1951. Ugo Tamarozzi is second from the left and Glauco Zitelli on the far right. *(Museo Ducati)*

RACING CUCCIOLOS

Following the end of World War Two there was an acute shortage of personal transportation in Italy. So in June 1946 Ducati, struggling to rebuild after the devastation of Allied bombing, entered into an agreement with SIATA of Turin to manufacture their Cucciolo, or 'Puppy'. This was a 48cc four-stroke engine that could be attached to a bicycle, and proved immediately successful. Designed by lawyer Aldo Farinelli and adopted by SIATA, the Cucciolo was the first new automotive design to appear in post-war Europe. By 1947 Ducati was under government control, and soon they took the SIATA licence and concentrated solely on Cucciolo production. The original T1 became the T2 in 1948, and the 60cc T3 by 1949.

As racing was endemic in Italy it was inevitable that the Cucciolo would be adapted for competition in the Micromotore class for machines up to 50cc. In February 1947 Mario Recchia gave the Cucciolo its first victory, and for 1948 Ducati offered their first racing engine, a T2 Sport to special order, with an oversized 8.9:1 piston giving a full 50cc. The power was increased from 1.2bhp at 4,250rpm to 2bhp at 5,700rpm. The T2 Sport was considerably successful during 1948, particularly in hill climbs, where its four-stroke torque provided an advantage over the two-stroke opposition, but also on street circuits. All Cucciolo racers at this stage featured proprietary frames as it wasn't until 1950 that Ducati produced their first complete motorcycle. This was designed in conjunction with Aero Caproni of Trento, but soon Caproni decided to build a similar Capriolo, threatening the market dominance of the Cucciolo.

Ducati officially entered competition for the first time by assisting Ugo Tamarozzi in his attempt on a series of world records at Monza on 5 March 1950. The 56-year-old Tamarozzi prepared the machine in his cellar in Milan, and with a 9.5:1 compression ratio and a 12mm Dell'Orto carburettor, and a 50/50 petrol/benzol fuel mixture, he scrupulously observed a 3,500rpm limit to set six distance and six speed records. His fastest record was the 100 miles (160.9km) at 66.092kmh (41.076mph). Not content with this, on 16 May Tamarozzi returned with a co-rider, Glauco Zitelli, and a full factory machine prepared by chief engineer Giovanni Fiorio, setting a further 20 records. The Cucciolo ran for 12 hours at 67.156kmh (41.738mph). On 13 November 1950 Tamarozzi and a team of riders including Alberto Farnè, Ettore Maini, Aldo Caroli, Gaetano Pennati, and Salvatore Sozzani, set a further 27 long-distance world records. These included the 3,000 kilometres (1,854.5 miles) at 66.320kmh (41.218mph) and the 48-hour at 63.200kmh (39.279mph), and the records stood for nearly five years.

During 1951 the factory persevered with the Cucciolo and 65 Sport in competition, and were rewarded with Franco Petrucci's third in the under-75cc class in the Milano–Taranto road race. The little engine was also suited to off-road competition. A factory team was entered in the ISDT held at the Valli Bergamasche in Italy that year, and Tamarozzi earned a silver medal. With the release of the overhead valve 98 in 1952 Ducati decided to concentrate on the 100cc racing category but had little success until Taglioni supervised their preparation for the 1954 ISDT held in Wales. Although the smallest machines entered in the event, Alberto Farnè and Giovanni Malaguti both won silver medals. In the 1954 Motogiro d'Italia Ducati entered five 98s. However, the Laverdas humbled Gandossi, Landi, Saccomandi, Recchia, and the young Franco Farnè.

THE MARIANNA

Taglioni always worked with surprising speed and showed a remarkable ability to get designs right the first time. Few designs exemplified this more than the Gran Sport, later nicknamed the Marianna (possibly because the Catholic Church celebrated 1955 as the 'Holy Year of Mary'). The Marianna was not only an advanced engine design, but it was conceived for racing first and production second. Thus it proved virtually unbeatable in the Italian road races, and formed the basis of the Grand Prix desmodromic racers and a range of racing and production machines through until 1974. Many of its design criteria carried through to the later 90° V-twins, and even the current Desmoquattro owes much to the Marianna. This was truly one of Ducati's great racing engines.

The basis of the Gran Sport engine was its vertically-split aluminium unit construction sand-cast crankcase. The cylinder (with cast-iron liner) was inclined forward 10° and a single overhead camshaft was driven by a set of straight-cut bevel gears. In an era where nearly all the competition featured pushrod valve operation this immediately gave the Gran Sport an advantage and was a reflection on the quality of machinery just installed at the Ducati factory. All the bearings were ball or roller, the crankshaft featuring full circle flywheels with a stepped crankpin (32mm on the rollers and 27mm at the ends). A feature that would carry through on all racing Ducati engines until the Pantah was a forged steel con-rod with dual strengthening ribs around both the small and big-end. On the Gran Sport the gudgeon diameter was 14mm. The bore and stroke of 49.4 x 52mm provided 99.66cc, and the forged three-ring piston gave a moderate 8.5:1 compression ratio.

Incorporated in the crankcases was a four-speed gearbox, driven by straight-cut primary gears with a wet multi-plate clutch. There was battery and coil ignition with the points driven off the lower bevel gear on the right, and the cylinder head was in two pieces. The 31 and 27mm valves were opposed at 80° and closed by exposed hairpin valve springs. Valve springs were notoriously prone to breakage, so each rider was supplied a valve spring compression tool to facilitate quick replacement. With a 20mm Dell'Orto carburettor mounted with a 15° downdraft, the first Gran Sport produced 9bhp at 9,000rpm. It was also extremely economical, providing more than 100mpg (2.82l/100km) at racing speeds.

This engine was placed in a single downtube tubular steel frame that utilised it as a stressed member, another feature of many future racing Ducatis. On the first Marianna the engine was located by separate plates to the frame, there were 17-inch wheels, and suspension was by telescopic forks with twin shock absorbers. The brakes were magnesium Amadoro, the wheelbase was only 1,283mm (4ft 2.5in), and the dry weight 80kg (176lb). To comply with Italian FMI regulations there was also a generator, horn, and headlamp, and instead of an air pump a compressed air canister sat on the left rear frame tube. With a top speed around 130kmh (81mph) the Marianna immediately looked a more promising race contender than its overhead valve predecessor.

Initial tests of a prototype Gran Sport at Modena in February 1955 were extremely encouraging, its speed also surprising representatives from rival factories. It was officially unveiled on 5 March, and, virtually untested, a total of 37 Gran Sports and ohv 98s were entered in the Motogiro d'Italia of 17–25 April. Riders included Gianni Degli Antoni, Leopoldo Tartarini, Francesco Villa, Antonio Graziano, Ettore Scamandri, Franco Farnè, and Giuliano Maoggi. Several younger riders were also provided with Mariannas. As told by Bruno Spaggiari, 'Taglioni and Montano sent letters to all their dealers and selected 25 from 200 candidates. I received a Marianna and this was my Ducati debut.' Following a blessing and Mass at the factory by Cardinal Lercaro the team was well prepared.

After the humiliation of the previous year no one could have predicted the success of the Marianna in the third Motogiro d'Italia of 1955. Mariannas won every inter-city stage, with Degli Antoni taking six, and Villa, Tartarini, and Graziano one each. Twenty-eight Ducatis completed the 3,400km (2,113 mile) event and Degli Antoni easily won the 100cc class at an average speed of 98.90kmh (61.47mph). This was 12.47kmh

Fabio Taglioni in retirement in 1995, at home with his orchids. He was as enthusiastic about these as he was about motorcycles. *(Ian Falloon)*

FABIO TAGLIONI

When he came to Ducati on 1 May 1954, Fabio Taglioni already had a considerable reputation as a motorcycle engineer. Born on 10 September 1920, he hailed from Lugo, in the centre of the Emilia Romagna region, known for a rich automotive engineering tradition. Lugo was also the birthplace of World War One flying ace Francesco Baracca. Baracca had served with Fabio Taglioni's father, Biagio, and flew with a distinctive prancing horse symbol that was later to feature on both Enzo Ferrari's cars (from nearby Maranello) and Taglioni's early Grand Prix racers. Taglioni's interest in motorcycles began during the 1930s, and after sustaining a leg wound during World War Two he completed his engineering studies at Bologna University in three years instead of the usual five by teaching himself. Graduating in 1948, he taught at a technical college in Imola and with the help of his pupils designed a racing 75, selling this to the small Bolognese motorcycle company Ceccato. This eventually led to his appointment as an assistant to Alfonso Drusiani at FB Mondial in 1952, an experience that would shape Taglioni's future. Mondial had just won three consecutive 125cc World Championships and Drusiani's double overhead camshaft racing 125 undoubtedly served as an inspiration for Taglioni when he came to design the Gran Sport.

From then on Taglioni worked only at Ducati. Though his success with the desmodromic Grand Prix racers provided him with an international reputation he remained loyal to Ducati. Even through the difficult decade of the 1960s when he was unable to race, Taglioni resisted the temptation to accept lucrative offers of work in the automobile industry. His friend Enzo Ferrari said, 'The door is always open,' and often Taglioni would use the resources of Maranello when he needed to. The author was fortunate to meet with Fabio Taglioni on many occasions and discuss his life with Ducati. Asked to name his favourite design, Taglioni replied, 'The 125 Desmo of 1957 and the 750 twin.' Of all the riders with whom he was associated, two stood out: 'Mike Hailwood, numero uno, and Gianni Degli Antoni.' When it came to other engineers it was Norton's Joe Craig who most influenced Taglioni. Although a prolific designer, with over 1,000 drawings to his credit, Taglioni was primarily interested in racing, often to the detriment of the production models. His formula for a racing machine called for 'light weight, simplicity, a narrow engine, and a wide power band.'

What was most impressive about Fabio Taglioni was his humility. He was never arrogant or dogmatic, and always acknowledged the support of others. Although sometimes criticised for his conservatism and reluctance to adopt new technology, Taglioni remains the premier figure in the history of Ducati racing. He was the father of the Desmodromic valve gear, and the only one to make it work successfully on a motorcycle. Even after his official retirement in 1989 Taglioni was involved in engine development, including the Cagiva F4. Later in life he suffered emphysema, the result of a lifetime of smoking, and had severe difficulty in talking. Fabio Taglioni nevertheless remained a revered figure at Borgo Panigale right up until his death on 19 July 2001, and every time a desmodromic Ducati wins a race his legacy continues.

With its single overhead camshaft driven by a vertical shaft and bevel gears, Taglioni's Marianna formed the basis of all single cylinder racing Ducatis. *(Ian Falloon)*

(7.75mph) faster than the Laverda class record set the previous year and good enough to place Degli Antoni fifth overall. Completing Ducati's triumph were Villa, Fantuzzi, Spaggiari, Maoggi, and Scamandri, taking the next five places. In the process the 100cc Mariannas beat all the 125s. Not only was Taglioni's future assured, but Ducati was able to advertise itself as 'the miracle of the Motogiro'. The Marianna was available as a catalogued model but was always an expensive limited edition production racer.

Success continued for Degli Antoni and the Marianna. On 8 May, ten days after the Motogiro, Degli Antoni led home Villa and Franco Farnè in the 100cc race at Imola. However, with the Milano–Taranto race looming in June Taglioni prepared a 125cc Marianna for Maoggi. The engine was bored to 55.3mm (the first oversquare Ducati engine), giving 124.8cc, and with a 22mm Dell'Orto carburettor the power was increased slightly to 10.5bhp at 9,800rpm. With 18-inch wheels the weight was increased to 85kg (187lb). Still, this wasn't enough for Maoggi to beat his teammate Degli Antoni on the 100 Marianna, Degli Antoni finishing 16th overall behind a field of Gilera Grand Prix 500 fours and MotoBi 250s. His average speed was 103.172kmh (64.122mph) and Ducatis took the first seven places in the 100cc class. Maoggi won the 125 category, but finished 21st overall.

With convincing victories in the long-distance road races, Ducati then turned to the various shorter events often held on street circuits around Italian cities. Francesco Villa won the 100cc Italian Championship and Degli Antoni a string of road races from Lugo to Fermo. Even privateers found the Marianna competitive and at the end of May Marcello Danna rode a streamlined 100cc Marianna to victory in the 'Race to the Sea' along the autostrada between Rome and Ostia. He averaged 122.449kmh (76.103mph).

As the debut racing season proved even more successful than anticipated Taglioni was allowed to develop the Gran Sport with a double overhead camshaft for 1956. This was the Bialbero, but as success was still vital in the Motogiro and Milano–Taranto, the single overhead camshaft Marianna was also refined, in both 100cc and 125cc versions. With a higher compression ratio of 9.7:1, the 100 now produced 10.5bhp at 9,800rpm, while the 125 made 14bhp at 10,000rpm. After a special blessing of riders, engineers, and bikes at the San Petronius cathedral in Bologna, the Ducati team under Dott. Eugenio Lolli managed to better the results of 1955. Giuliano Maoggi went on to win the event outright on his 125, beating all the 175s. Teammate Maranghi took second with Artusi, Montanari, and Falconi filling out the 125 class. Again the 100cc Marianna

Below left: The team line-up for a special mass at the factory prior to the 1955 Motogiro. On the far left is Degli Antoni, with Spaggiari and Farnè on the far right. *(Walter Breveglieri)*

Below right: Leopoldo Tartarini rode the 100cc Marianna in the 1955 Giro d'Italia, winning one stage. On the rear frame tube is the compressed air pump. *(Walter Breveglieri)*

Top: The Siluro on the banking at Monza in November 1956, on the way to setting 46 speed records. *(Museo Ducati)*

Bottom: Carini and Ciceri received assistance from the factory in their record attempt. On the left is the ever-present Farnè. *(Museo Ducati)*

THE SILURO (TORPEDO)

As speed and distance records were an extremely popular source of publicity in the 1950s, two Milanese riders, Mario Carini and Santo Ciceri, encouraged Ducati to support them in a record attempt at Monza on 30 November 1956. Ciceri had only recently won at Modena on a 100cc Marianna, and Carini had some success with Mondials, so Ducati agreed to prepare the engine and commission aluminium streamlining from the Milanese company Nardi and Danese. With the aid of a wind tunnel, the design featured an open cockpit and a small Plexiglas screen, and was extremely effective. Supported by additional tubing, underneath the aluminium bodywork was a virtually standard 100cc Marianna. The only engine change was a Dell'Orto SS 25mm carburettor.

Despite the threat of rain, Carini and Ciceri set a total of 44 new records, and the 100cc Marianna was timed at 171.910kmh (106.843mph). They took 13 records in the 100 class, 13 in the 125, 13 in the 175, and five in the 250. Distance records included 50km at 164.443kmh (102.202mph) and 1,000km in just under six and a half hours at 154.556kmh (96.057mph). Not only had the Marianna proved its speed and reliability, but as these records were previously held by DEMM, Guazzoni, Lambretta, and Moto Guzzi, it was a triumph for Ducati and Fabio Taglioni.

Above left: Marcello Sestini on the 125 Marianna in the final Motogiro of 1957. (Walter Breveglieri)

Above right: Antonio Graziano rides through the snow during the 1956 Motogiro. (Walter Breveglieri)

Oposite: The Bialbero was essentially a Marianna apart from the cylinder head. From 1957 there was a one-piece cylinder head casting. (Ian Falloon)

swamped the smaller category, Gandossi leading home Villa, Spaggiari, Geminiani, Scamandri, and Farnè. Mariannas also took out every stage of the race.

Results were similar in the final Milano–Taranto race, held on 10 June. Here Degli Antoni astounded everyone by finishing sixth overall on a 125 Marianna at 103.176kmh (64.124mph), ahead of most of the 500s and 250s. Gandossi won the 100cc class at 99.744kmh (61.991mph). The dominance of the Marianna also continued in domestic events, Franco Farnè winning the 100cc Junior Italian Championship. Later in the year the Marianna Gran Sport engine grew to 175cc. With a bore and stroke of 62 x 57.8mm, and Dell'Orto 22.5mm SS carburettor, the 175 produced 16bhp at 9,000rpm, but only appeared in a few events towards the end of 1956. Not very successful, it was replaced by the 175 F3.

As the Milano–Taranto was cancelled following a tragedy during the Mille Miglia in May (when De Portago's Ferrari 315 had run off the road and killed nine spectators), the Motogiro d'Italia held from 6–14 April 1957 was the final Italian road race. Again the Mariannas dominated, winning every 100cc stage and eight 125 stages. Mariannas occupied the first seven places in both classes, Mandolini winning the 100cc category and Graziano the 125. Even after the end of the Gran Fondo races the Marianna was still raced with success, notably in the Montjuich 24-hour race at Barcelona in July 1957. On a 125 intended for the Milano–Taranto, Spaggiari and Gandossi won the event outright at an average speed of 57.660mph (92.775kmh), with Farnè and Mandolini second and Relats and Roda third on similar machines. In 1958 Mandolini and Maranghi led home another Marianna domination, Ducatis filling the first five places. Farnè and Villa were second, with Ricardo Fargas and Jaime Caralt third.

During 1957 a special 241cc Marianna was produced for Pierfrancesco Leopardi and raced at Riva del Garda. The 73 x 57.8mm engine produced around 20bhp and would form the basis for the later 250s. Even well after the release of the 125 F3, Mariannas remained favoured mounts in Italy. Maoggi continued to race his 125 Marianna up until 1959, and Francesco Villa had success on a Marianna as late as 1962.

THE 125 GRAND PRIX (BIALBERO)

The mid-1950s were golden years for the Italian motorcycle industry, and following the success of its Marianna Ducati grew to become one of the largest motorcycle manufacturers in Italy. Production levels were around 20,000 a year and employees numbered more than 700, so there was justification for an escalation of racing development. Not content with their victories in the MSDS (macchine sport derivate dalla serie) category for production sports machines, Montano and Taglioni wanted to win the modified sports machine class. For this Taglioni created the Bialbero, or double camshaft 125 Grand Prix, officially unveiled on 25 February 1956.

Essentially a Gran Sport apart from the cylinder head, the twin overhead camshaft layout immediately provided 15.5bhp at 10,500rpm. With harsh winter conditions restricting testing, Taglioni still managed to raise the power to 16bhp, and maximum revs to 11,500rpm. Early examples featured a Marianna-derived two-piece cylinder head but this was problematic with the relatively high 9.8:1 compression ratio and high lift camshafts (7.5mm inlet and 7.0mm). However, despite casting the head and cambox together the Bialbero was still considerably down on power compared to the works MVs. With a handlebar fairing and streamlined seat the top speed was around 170kmh (105mph). Taglioni also included a fifth gear outside the crankcase wall, behind the clutch inside the primary drive case on the early prototype, and this was incorporated in all Bialberos. The basic chassis was that of a Marianna, but even in the hands of Degli Antoni and veteran Alano Montanari the early Bialbero was outclassed in Italian Championship events in 1956. Degli Antoni gave the fully-faired Bialbero its debut at Faenza in May, but finished second to Ubbiali's MV.

Immediately after the Bialbero's debut, Taglioni turned to desmodromics on the factory machines. However, the Bialbero continued to be developed alongside the Desmo and was made available to privateers in limited quantities. Franco Villa also raced an official Bialbero in Italian events. For 1957 the modified sports category became Formula 2, still requiring the standard 22mm carburettor, but for open events the Bialbero was fitted with either a 26 or 27mm Dell'Orto SS1 carburettor. There was a new cylinder head casting with a distinctive (and beautiful) polished alloy gear cover, and an additional oil supply direct to the camshafts. The frame now incorporated developments from the desmodromic 125, including a dual loop subframe under the engine for additional strength. With dustbin fairings allowed that year the magnesium Amadoro brakes (180 x 40mm on the front and 160 x 40mm on the rear) featured large forward scoops reaching underneath the axles. The forks were 30mm, and wheels 18-inch. With a wheelbase of only 1,219mm (4ft), and a dry weight of 90kg (198lb), the Bialbero was a tiny motorcycle and really only suited smaller riders.

By 1958 many of the developments of the Desmo had also appeared on the Bialbero. There were new crankcases and a dual cradle frame with upward sloping top frame tubes. The engine also featured a new cylinder head casting, and twin spark plug ignition with two 3-volt coils and a 6-volt battery under the seat. The Marianna generator was removed and the ignition was total loss. By the end of 1958 the power was up to 17bhp at 12,000rpm and the top speed around 175kmh (109mph). Because there was no longer a large dustbin fairing the Amadoro brakes were smaller (180 x 25mm) with twin forward air scoops. As always the official factory machines were more highly developed. According to Villa his Bialbero produced 18.5 horsepower at 12,800rpm.

As a privateer racer the 125 Bialbero was incredibly successful. In England, Fron Purslow won a succession of races during 1958, which continued with Mike Hailwood after he purchased the machine. 125 Championship victories were scored from 1957 to 1959 in countries as diverse as Holland, Switzerland, Brazil, Venezuela, and Sweden. After the factory officially retired from Grand Prix racing at the end of 1959 some of the works 125 Desmos had their desmo cylinder heads substituted with Bialbero cylinder heads, and there were also some Bialberos with Formula 3 crankcases. Sold to privateers, these were raced successfully for many more years.

Right: Many of the later Bialbero's features were shared with the Desmo, including the Amadoro brakes and dual loop subframe under the engine. *(Ian Falloon)*

THE 'KAVANAGH SPECIAL' AND THE 220

During 1959 the factory racing programme was scaled down significantly, and apart from Mike Hailwood the only sponsored foreign rider was Australian Ken Kavanagh. Kavanagh was an ex-factory Norton and Moto Guzzi rider residing in Bergamo and was provided with a special 125 Bialbero to race in selected Grands Prix. This Bialbero (number 123, or the 'Kavanagh Special') shared more with the final large crankcase 125 Desmo (Barcone), also featuring an integral six-speed gearbox. Unlike the Desmo Barcone the cylinder was vertical, the top crankcase line was horizontal, and it had a special double downtube full cradle frame. On this one-off machine Kavanagh won the Finnish Grand Prix at Helsinki in May, as well as races at Turku.

At the end of 1959 Kavanagh decided to return to Australia for the first time since 1951 and to race in some events during the summer. He wanted to take the 125 'special' and something suitable for the 250 class. As Kavanagh had acted as interpreter for the Berliners (Ducati's US distributors) on their visit to Italy in October 1959, Montano was grateful and agreed to supply a special 220. Montano also reasoned that it could be good publicity and would assist in finding an Australian distributor. As Kavanagh recounted, 'Taglioni calculated that with a modified 175 F3 he could get enough power to defeat the only competition, a couple of NSU Sportmaxs.' Within two weeks a team of rider-testers including Farnè, Francesco Villa, Spaggiari, and Mario Recchia, had created the machine. A special 9:1 69mm piston was machined from a blank, but 'it was weak, with the top ring too high and the piston crown too thin,' recalled Kavanagh. With an experimental Bialbero cylinder head and straight-cut bevel gears, the 216.13cc engine produced nearly 28bhp at 9,600rpm, but 'the carburation from the 29mm SS1 Dell'Orto was terrible,' Kavanagh continued, 'and although we planned a five-speed gearbox there was no time to machine one so we had to settle for the 175 F3 four-speed.' The front brake was the same Amadoro as fitted to the 125 Grand Prix, and the one-piece fairing was borrowed from Franco Villa's 125.

Both the 125 and the 220 (number 522) were shipped to Australia in November, with the first race at Phillip Island on 1 January 1960. Here Kavanagh won the 125 race, but the 220 retired with carburettor flooding. However, at Fisherman's Bend on 14 February Kavanagh

Ken Kavanagh had a special six-speed 125 Bialbero during 1959. He took this machine to Australia and won the 125 race at Phillip Island on New Year's day 1960. (Mick Woollett Collection)

won both races, even with a broken coupling on the bevel gear driveshaft (a recurring problem). The series then went down to Tasmania in March and with the 125 and 250 races run concurrently at Longford Eric Hinton rode the 220 to victory with Kavanagh again winning on the 125. At Symmonds Plains Kavanagh was again unbeatable, taking a further victory on the 220. After unsuccessfully trying to sell both machines in Australia for £1,000, they ended up in England. Jim Redman purchased the 125 and raced it at the Isle Of Man in 1960, finishing 13th. The success of the 220 prompted the factory to produce a few similar machines during 1960, now with a five-speed gearbox.

2 DESMODROMICS

Fabio Taglioni, the father of the Desmo, pictured here in 1959 with the desmodromic 125 single. *(Mick Woollett Collection)*

Although the 125 Bialbero offered improved performance over the Marianna, its reliability was questionable at high rpm. Valve-to-piston clearance was critical with the higher compression ratios now required, compounded by the problem of valve float and the wide included valve angle of 80°. Taglioni had shown interest in desmodromic, or positive valve actuation, during his days at university, and had even proposed a desmodromic system while at Mondial in 1953. Mondial's conservative Count Boselli wouldn't permit Taglioni to pursue this path, but it was different at Ducati. Almost as soon as he joined the company he began to work on a desmodromic cylinder head for the Gran Sport, and during 1955 produced the first desmodromic prototype. Taglioni's faith in the concept was also reassured by the success of the desmodromic Mercedes W196 Grand Prix and 300 SLR sports cars during 1954 and 1955.

Unlike the Mercedes desmodromic system, which used a single overhead camshaft with scissor rockers operating the valves, Taglioni went for a triple overhead camshaft (Trialbero) layout, with two outside opening camshafts (like the Bialbero) and a central camshaft closing the valves through forked rockers. Light closing rocker return springs were initially fitted but were later discarded when it was found they were unnecessary. The actual cylinder head design was similar to the Bialbero, with a 31mm inlet and 27mm exhaust valve set, still set at the wide 80° included angle, but the

Desmo had considerably higher valve lift with 8.1mm inlet and 7.4mm exhaust. Drive to the three camshafts was the usual straight-cut bevel gear and 15mm vertical shaft, but the shaft was waisted to vary the engine's torque characteristics. A shaft diameter of 11mm (the safe minimum) provided peak torque at 8,000rpm while a shaft diameter of 14.8mm (maximum) gave a higher torque peak. With the narrower shaft retarding the valve timing in relation to piston position this was an early form of variable valve timing.

The original Desmo had a single 14mm spark plug but an additional 10mm plug on the right soon supplemented this. As with the Bialbero there was no generator and ignition was total loss with two 3-volt

coils. As the combustion chamber design was arguably obsolete early single spark plug examples required considerable ignition advance of 42°, but the twin plug ignition enabled this to be cut back to a more reasonable 36°. The inlet port was 27mm and carburation generally by a 27mm Dell'Orto, increased to 29mm for fast circuits or reduced to 23 or even 22mm on tighter tracks. Initial power output was only marginally increased over the Bialbero at 17bhp at 12,500rpm, but with a much higher safety margin. The little Desmo could be run to 14,000rpm on the overrun, assisting engine braking, but necessitating continual crankshaft replacement.

Below the cylinder head the early desmodromic engine was virtually identical to the Bialbero, with a five-speed gearbox (the fifth still inside the primary drive case), and a bore and stroke of 55.25 x 52mm. The sand-cast crankcases still featured a blanked off kick-start boss. The cast (not forged) three-ring piston provided a compression ratio of 10:1 and there was a similar 107mm steel con-rod, with a 16mm gudgeon and stepped crankpin, 30mm on the rollers and 25 at the ends. The big-end bearing cage was steel with the crankshaft flywheels forged integrally with the mainshaft and heavily machined. Unlike the Bialbero, though, the ball main bearings were an axial thrust type, loaded by a large star washer between the drive-side bearing and flywheel. The earliest desmo engines were installed in a chassis that was similar to the Bialbero but incorporated additional lower strengthening tubes under the engine. The brakes were also magnesium Amadoro, with large cooling intakes for the Nardi-designed dustbin fairing used in 1956.

Ducati's goal at the beginning of 1956 was to acquit themselves at the Nations Grand Prix at Monza in September, so, in preparation for this important event, the Desmo's debut took place unannounced at the non-championship Swedish Grand Prix at Hedemora on 15 July. In the hands of Taglioni's star rider Degli Antoni the 125 Desmo easily won the 125cc race. By the 14th lap Degli Antoni had overtaken the entire field, winning at an average speed of 84.45mph (135.88kmh) with a fastest lap of 87.56mph (140.88kmh). Not only was Taglioni's desmodromic system vindicated, but a host of private MVs and Mondials were soundly beaten in the process.

After the magnificent debut in Sweden, disaster struck during testing at Monza prior to the Nations Grand Prix. Rounding the Lesmo curve Degli Antoni lost control and was killed. Although Alberto Gandossi was drafted in as a replacement the pall cast by Degli Antoni's death proved too much and the three Desmos were swamped by Ubbiali's MV. Artusi came fourth, and Gandossi seventh, but it was obvious that the team was disillusioned. Although the Desmo would be raced in Italian events during 1957, it was decided to wait until 1958 before seriously contesting Grands Prix.

During the winter Taglioni managed to increase the power of the Desmo to 18bhp, still at 12,500rpm. Earlier he had also produced a 100cc (49.4 x 58mm) Marianna-

Left: The triple camshaft desmodromic cylinder head sat on top of Bialbero crankcases. Here Mario Recchia works on a 125 Desmo at the 1958 Dutch Grand Prix. *(Mick Woollett)*

Opposite: Alano Montanari also rode the 125 Desmo during 1956. During 1956 and 1957 the factory Desmos ran full dustbin fairings, and the riders generally wore helmets with matching stripes. *(Museo Ducati)*

Right: Gianni Degli Antoni, Ducati's leading rider of 1955 and 1956, pictured here at the start of the 1955 Motogiro. Taglioni believed he could have won the 125 World Championship. *(Walter Breveglieri)*

Opposite: Dave Chadwick lines up alongside Romolo Ferri at the start of the 1958 125 Grand Prix at the Isle of Man. The Desmos had full double cradle frames this year. *(Mick Woollett)*

GIANNI DEGLI ANTONI

Although his racing career with Ducati was only brief, few riders made the impact of Giovanni (Gianni) Degli Antoni. Born in 1932, Degli Antoni was a former mechanic for the Stanguellini racing car team and took up racing motorcycles with the MV Agusta Junior squad. During 1954 he came to the attention of Taglioni and was signed as an official Squadra Ducati rider for 1955. Soon his combination of outstanding riding ability and technical knowledge saw him as Ducati's team leader and chief development rider. Taglioni valued him so highly that Degli Antoni even missed the vital 1956 Motogiro to concentrate on development of the Bialbero and Trialbero Desmo. Degli Antoni's death on 7 August 1956 was not only devastating to the team, but resulted in a loss of morale that would affect them for several months.

based version in preparation for 1957, the final year of the Italian Formula 2 class. Bruno Spaggiari first raced this at Modena in October 1956, and with an 11:1 compression ratio it produced 12bhp at 13,000rpm. There was no fairing and the top speed was around 140kmh (87mph). In the hands of Franco Farnè the 100 Desmo dominated the 1957 Italian Junior Championship.

During 1957 Taglioni also continued to develop the 125 Desmo, now with forged Mahle pistons and nimonic valves to improve reliability. The power was increased to 19bhp at 13,000rpm and Bruno Spaggiari rode it with some success in Italian events. The Nations Grand Prix at Monza was the only Grand Prix outing for the Desmos that year, but this again was a disappointment. On the first lap Gandossi fell, bringing down a third of the field in the process. Things could only improve, but Taglioni was confident. He also had a 125cc twin ready in case the single was outclassed. Romolo Ferri's performance on the Gilera 125cc twin during 1956 pointed an alternative way for the future.

THE 1958 SEASON

With the retirement of Moto Guzzi, Mondial, and Gilera at the end of 1957, the 1958 Grand Prix season shaped up as a contest between Ducati and MV. Carlo Ubbiali and reigning champion Tarquinio Provini were formidable opponents and in April Ducati announced a 14-man team. This year there were Senior and Junior Championships in Italy, with Farnè leading the assault on the Junior title and Spaggiari and Gandossi attempting the Senior. For the Grands Prix the team would be expanded to include Ferri, Francesco Villa, Luigi Taveri, Dave Chadwick, and, for the Isle of Man, Sammy Miller. For 1958 the Desmo single featured new crankcases, strengthened at the rear to provide a support for the twin rear engine plates. Some were also six-speed, with the extra gear sandwiched with the fifth gear between the clutch and gearbox wall. The frames were double-cradle, and Ferri's featured a lowered steering head, bent downtubes, and shorter forks to accommodate his small stature. There were either full race dolphin or smaller half fairings this year, and Amadoro brakes with upper or lower air scoops.

The season began promisingly with Farnè, Gandossi,

Chadwick finished third in the 1958 Isle of Man GP, behind Ferri and the MV of Ubbiali. *(Mick Woollett)*

and Spaggiari convincingly beating the MVs in the opening rounds of the Italian Championship. Then it was to the Isle of Man on 4 June, staged on the shorter 10.79-mile (17.36km) Clypse Circuit. Unfortunately Gandossi was sidelined following a road bike accident, but the speed of the Desmos was evident, with Taveri leading until his piston rings broke (a continual problem with the high revving Desmo). Ubbiali's brilliance gave him victory on the MV, but he was chased home by the Desmos of Ferri, Chadwick, and Miller. Post-race strip-downs confirmed that while Taveri's machine was six-speed, all the other Desmos were five-speed.

At the next Grand Prix at Assen Taveri battled with Ubbiali, only to be beaten by 0.2 seconds at the finish. However, Ducatis filled out six places in the top ten and showed they were a real force in Grand Prix racing. A new higher lift camshaft for the ultra-fast Belgian Grand Prix in July gave the Desmo extra speed over the MV and Gandossi provided Ducati with their first Grand Prix victory. Averaging 157.860kmh (98.111mph), Gandossi led Ferri in second, Chadwick in fourth, and Taveri in sixth place. The MVs were truly outclassed and it had been a magnificent day for Ducati.

Unfortunately the season was marked by misfortune and injury. Spaggiari injured himself in a crash at Alessandria in June, and at the next Grand Prix at the Nürburgring Ferri also crashed badly, prematurely ending his racing career. On top of that Taveri's Desmo broke its crankshaft and Gandossi's threw a con-rod. The MVs were back on top, at least until the next Grand Prix at Hedemora in Sweden.

At the same venue where Degli Antoni had provided a stunning debut victory, the Desmos were again invincible. Gandossi led Taveri home at 146kmh (91mph), 10kmh (6.2mph) faster than Degli Antoni's speed only two years earlier. Taglioni's little Desmo had come a long way in a short time and Gandossi went into the penultimate Grand Prix at Ulster in August with a chance of still winning the title. In mist and rain Gandossi leaped away, only to crash at Leathemstown. Although he remounted to finish fourth, Ubbiali won the championship. It was not so much that Ducati had lost as Ubbiali had won. There was some consolation, though, as the next day Farnè sealed the Italian Junior title, and the cancellation of the final round of the Senior Championship saw Spaggiari confirmed as Senior Italian Champion.

With the World Championship lost Ducati went to the final Grand Prix at Monza on 5 September determined to at least gain some national kudos. A huge effort was made, with Franco Villa debuting the new 125 Desmo twin, and Desmo singles provided for Gandossi, Taveri, Chadwick, and Spaggiari (returning from injury). Continual development to the singles saw more sculptured crankcases and a dual cradle frame with the rear engine mount held by tubes rather than metal plates. According to Bruno Spaggiari, 'Monza 1958 was my first Grand Prix and the first time I rode a six-speed Desmo. There was also one of the revised large crankcase six-speed machines [ie a Barcone] available.' In the race Spaggiari rode the ex-Ferri machine, and the Nations Grand Prix at Monza was a memorable day for him. In front of 100,000 enthusiastic spectators he led Ducatis home in the first five places. The mighty MVs were humiliated as Spaggiari won at an average speed of 155.827kmh (96.847mph). For Taglioni and his racing team it was a spectacular way to end the season.

THE 1959 AND 1960 SEASONS

Emphasis on developing the production range of overhead camshaft singles saw a considerably reduced racing effort for the 1959 season. Rather than full-time factory involvement, Desmo singles were loaned to a selection of riders for various events. Apart from Hailwood, singles were also supplied to Spaggiari and Villa, while Taveri had a twin. Ken Kavanagh and Alberto Pagani received Bialberos. Kavanagh purchased his and was provided with a desmo cylinder head and a factory mechanic for selected events. For 1959 all the Desmo singles were six-speed, and initially Hailwood had two 1958 models (the ex-Ferri Nations GP winner and Taveri's) with a double cradle frame. The Barcone (Barge), incorporating the six-speed gearbox inside the crankcases, was also developed during the season. The cylinder was still inclined forward, unlike Kavanagh's similar Bialbero (as described in the previous chapter). At the Isle of Man TT, again held on the shorter Clypse circuit, Hailwood and Villa turned up with Desmo twins, but Hailwood opted to race the single. Spaggiari

Left: One of the greatest road racers of all time, Mike Hailwood began his Grand Prix career with Ducati. Here the 18-year-old Hailwood is about to test the 175 twin at Brands Hatch in early 1959. *(Mick Woollett)*

Opposite: Two Desmo 125s at the line up for the 1958 Dutch Grand Prix at Assen. Although Taveri narrowly lost the race, Desmos filled out the minor places. *(Mick Woollett)*

MIKE HAILWOOD

Arguably the greatest motorcycle road racer of all time, Stanley Michael Bailey Hailwood was born on 2 April 1940 and was associated with Ducati at the beginning and end of his illustrious career. With the support of his wealthy father Stan, who established Ecurie Sportive to further Mike's racing, a 125 Bialbero was purchased from then British Ducati agent Fron Purslow during 1958. In the early days Mike seemed more interested in playing jazz than racing motorcycles and he suffered criticism through having a millionaire father who provided the best equipment and tuners. However, he quickly overcame this and established himself as an extraordinary talent.

Mike's first ride on the Bialbero was at the Dutch Grand Prix in June 1958, and he finished tenth. He went on to win three races on it that year before Stan visited Italy and arranged to take over the distribution of Ducati motorcycles in England. In return he was able to obtain a pair of factory 125 Desmo singles, and the services of mechanic Oscar Folesani, for the 1959 Grand Prix season. He was also provided with a factory-prepared 125 Desmo twin for selected events. Soon after receiving the Desmo single Hailwood rode it to victory at Snetterton on 29 March, the first win in England by a desmodromic Ducati. He followed this with 11 victories in England that year to easily win the British ACU 125 Championship. Hailwood had an extraordinary ability to ride any capacity of motorcycle and won all four British titles (125, 250, 350, and 500) in 1959 and 1960.

After 1960 Ecurie Sportive sold their Ducatis and Hailwood became a factory rider. He went on to win nine world championships on Hondas and MVs before turning his hand to car racing. Here he was also successful, winning the 1972 European Formula 2 Championship. Retiring to live in New Zealand in 1975, his ride on a Ducati 750 SS in the 1977 Australian Castrol Six-hour race sparked one of the most spectacular racing comebacks ever. He won the 1978 TT F1 race (see Chapter 5), returning to take out the Senior TT on a Suzuki RG500 in 1979. He and his daughter Michelle were tragically killed in a road accident near their home in Tamworth-in-Arden on 22 March 1981 when a truck driver made an illegal U-turn. Michelle was killed outright, and Mike succumbed to his injuries a few days later.

The Barcone was the final development of the 125 Desmo single and not only featured larger crankcases, but also a new frame. This is the machine raced by Kavanagh at the Isle of Man in 1960. It subsequently ended up with Ecurie Sportive. *(Ian Falloon)*

In addition to racing in Grands Prix, Hailwood rode the 125 Desmo single to victory in the 1959 British 125 Championship. Here he is at Aberdare Park, on his way to another victory. *(Mick Woollett)*

and Kavanagh also had Desmo singles, but they were outpaced by Provini's MV and Taveri's MZ. Hailwood finished third, Spaggiari retired, while Villa crashed the twin, badly damaging it.

Hailwood, Spaggiari, and Villa again rode Desmo singles at the next Grand Prix at Hockenheim, but again, despite Hailwood's efforts, the single was overwhelmed by the MVs. Hailwood again came third, with Villa and Spaggiari behind. When Hailwood set the fastest practice lap for the Dutch Grand Prix he looked set to win his first Grand Prix, leading the race before succumbing to stress fracture problems with the cast pistons. He finished third yet again, although Spaggiari came second. At Spa the following weekend Taveri was back with Ducati (on the 125 twin) and was fastest in practice but could only manage third in the race. Hailwood's piston broke, and at the Swedish Grand Prix he rode the 125 twin hoping for more speed. Only managing fourth, he reverted to the single at the next Grand Prix at Ulster. As the MVs didn't arrive in time, Hailwood won his first Grand Prix after a race-long dice with Gary Hocking and the MZ. Although he could only manage eighth at the final Grand Prix at Monza, Hailwood finished third in the 125 World Championship.

At the end of 1959 Ducati ceased their official involvement in Grand Prix racing and Stan Hailwood managed to acquire two 125 Desmo twins, a Barcone Desmo single (with another later in the season), and commissioned Taglioni to build two 250 twins and a 350 twin. Ducati again provided mechanic Folesani, specifically to help with the preparation of the under-developed twins. Built during the winter, the Barcone 125 was the final development of the single cylinder Desmo and was conceived to eventually become a full 250cc. The first example arrived at Ecurie Sportive early in 1960 and there was another for Kavanagh at the Isle of Man. These now had frames with a single downtube splitting into double cradle underneath the engine, and for Hailwood the team installed a reshaped fibreglass fairing instead of the factory aluminium type. Hailwood also used a taller fuel tank and more thickly padded seat, and immediately won nine 125 races prior to the Isle of Man TT. He was reported as delighted with the revised 125, which was much improved over the previous version.

The 125 twins arrived in May, and at the Isle of Man Hailwood had three temperamental Ducati twins in

Top: Although the desmodromic cylinder head was similar to earlier versions, the Barcone represented a major development. *(Ian Falloon)*

Bottom: The six-speed gearbox was now incorporated inside the crankcases. *(Ian Falloon)*

THE 125 DESMO BARCONE

Factory data released for these machines in 1962 stated that the maximum power was 21.8bhp at 11,800rpm and that the engine should run to 12,200rpm in sixth gear. Maximum rpm was 12,500. The valve timing was inlet opening 65° before top dead centre and closing 75° after bottom dead centre, with the exhaust opening 75° before bottom dead centre and closing 55° after top dead centre. Even with twin spark plugs the ignition advance was 47–50°. It was advised that the engine should be sent back to the factory at the end of the racing season to replace the cylinder and piston 'because we have specialists and special tools to do this job.'

their developmental stages to contend with. He found the 125 twin slower than the Barcone single, but elected to race the single and crashed on the first lap. The throttle cable broke on the 250 and the 350 handled so badly in practice he chose not to ride it. Kavanagh's 125 race ended when his rear wheel collapsed.

After the Isle of Man the factory Barcone Desmo raced by Kavanagh at the TT wound up with Ecurie Sportive, where it joined Hailwood's first 125 Barcone. One was used for short circuit British events, and the other was prepared for Grands Prix, it being standard practice for Ecurie Sportive to duplicate machinery. While the single was still competitive on British short circuits, it was totally outclassed in GPs. At the Dutch Grand Prix Hailwood finished eighth, and he elected to ride the 125 twin at Spa. Hailwood's final international event on the single was at Zaragoza in Spain in October, where he won the 125 race.

In England, though, Hailwood and the Barcone were proving a formidable combination and several more victories enabled him to take the 125 British Championship. At the end of the season, his original Barcone was returned to the factory. With a smaller fuel tank, an aluminium half fairing, and revised suspension, Franco Farnè raced this, and an earlier double-cradle frame type, under Scuderia Farnè-Stanzano in 1961. He won at Modena (on the earlier version), and at Cesenatico. For one of the most important events on the calendar, the Imola Gold Cup in April, Farnè rode the Barcone to a spectacular victory ahead of the factory Hondas of Tom Phillis and Jim Redman. Farnè's success on the Desmo Barcone even prompted Honda to produce their own desmodromic twin. Taveri rode it at Modena in 1962 but Honda then decided to pursue the path of multiple cylinders.

After Imola this Barcone may have returned to England, where Arthur Wheeler presumably raced it. At some stage it was also fitted with Oldani brakes and forks with internal springs. The fate of Hailwood's other Barcone (the ex-Kavanagh TT machine) is easier to trace. It was loaned to Fron Purslow at the end of 1960 and ridden by Taveri, Purslow, and Percy Tait during 1961. Tait won the British Championship at Oulton Park in August. Hailwood then sold the machine to the Dugdales in 1962, and eventually it found its way to Bob Schanz in the US in 1964.

Opposite, top: Tartarini with the 175 twin at the start of the 1957 Motogiro. Although it failed here it formed the basis for the 125 Desmo twin the following year. *(Museo Ducati)*

Opposite, bottom: Luigi Taveri sat on pole position for the 1959 Belgian Grand Prix on the 125 Desmo twin. He finished third. *(Mick Woollett)*

PARALLEL TWINS THE 175

Taglioni knew only too well that a single cylinder was limited in ultimate horsepower and as far back as 1950 had sketched a plan for a parallel twin. He eventually found the time to produce a 175 twin during 1956, and it was displayed at the Milan Show at the end of the year. Leopoldo Tartarini raced this in the 1957 Motogiro d'Italia but retired with ignition and generator problems during the third stage. The 175 established the basis for all racing parallel twins in that it featured twin overhead camshafts driven by a train of spur gears from a jackshaft between the cylinders. There was a pressed up crankshaft consisting of two flywheel assemblies clamped by Hirth (radially serrated) couplings. Complex and difficult to work on, the engines were beautifully constructed, with the flywheels and big-end assemblies machined from solid and all the gears drilled for lightness. There was dry clutch and exposed hairpin valve springs but still the wide 80° included valve angle. With an 11:1 compression ratio and 18mm Dell'Orto carburettors, the 49 x 46.6mm 175 produced 22bhp at 11,000rpm. By 1959 this was increased to around 25bhp but the powerband was too narrow, the 112kg (247lb) machine too heavy, and it suffered in comparison to the single. This early 175 featured Amadoro brakes with low front air scoops designed for a dustbin fairing, and for the Motogiro it had a larger fuel tank and horn.

Another 175 twin was produced during 1959 and sent to Mike Hailwood for evaluation. There was a new frame, rear suspension, and Amadoro brakes, and although Hailwood tested it at Brands Hatch in March he didn't race it. This machine was apparently sold to Arthur Wheeler, but Wheeler was apparently unhappy with it and it returned to Bologna. This example (with the revised frame) was acquired by the Berliners during 1959 and featured in their promotional literature. During 1964 one of the 175s was converted into a 250 by Franco Villa to use in the Italian Championship. However, Villa didn't end up racing it and the machine eventually went to the US, where it remains.

THE 125

Although unsuccessful, the 175 twin was a unique design that had a lot of potential, so when Taglioni decided to develop a 125cc racing twin he took the 175 as a basis and constructed desmodromic cylinder heads, with a similar triple camshaft set-up to the single. The two crankshafts moved in step and because of the complicated camshaft drive there was a wide 178mm spacing between the cylinders. With a bore and stroke of 42.5 x 45mm the engine was surprisingly undersquare for a Taglioni design, but it was still safe to an amazing 17,000rpm. The Mahle three-ring pistons gave a compression ratio of 10.2:1, there was a single 10mm spark plug per cylinder, and with special 23mm Dell'Orto carburettors with flat-sided float chambers the power was 22.5bhp at 13,800rpm. Development during 1959 eventually saw this rise to 26bhp at 14,000rpm, quite an astounding figure for a 125. However, the powerband was so narrow the machine was difficult to ride, despite its close ratio six-speed gearbox. A unique feature of the twin was the ability to remove one side of the engine while leaving the other intact. The frame was a twin-cradle type but the handling was suspect. Although the machine used 17-inch wheels during 1958, there were 18-inch wheels for 1959 to improve stability. Originally the Amadoro brakes were shared with the single but these were increased 10mm for 1959. Another disadvantage of the twin was its weight, a claimed 92kg (203lb) dry.

The 125 Desmo twin may have been a sophisticated design but this didn't translate into race success. The three third places at Monza (1958 and 1959) and Spa (1959), were its only significant results. Although Stan Hailwood claimed to have purchased all three examples prior to the Isle of Man, he could only have had two, as Franco Farnè continued to race a 125 twin throughout the 1960 season in Italy. The diminutive Farnè won at Monza in September 1960 on the 125 twin, but the larger framed Mike Hailwood couldn't come to terms with little machines (his best result was sixth in the 1960 Belgian Grand Prix). It was several years later, in Spain in 1965, that the 125 twin achieved its most success. At La Coruña, Bilbao, and Valladolid, Spaggiari won on a machine prepared by Mototrans. He raced it in some opening events in Italy in 1966 but by now Ducati was concentrating on developing the 250 Desmo single.

THE 250

During 1959 Stan Hailwood persuaded Ducati to produce a doubled version of the 125 Desmo single for the 250 class. As we have seen, Mike Hailwood always struggled to fit the smaller machines and Stan undoubtedly paid handsomely for this specially commissioned racer. The 250 shared its 55.25 x 52mm dimensions with the 125 single but in other respects it was a scaled-up 125 Desmo twin. It had a six-speed gearbox and twin Dell'Orto 30mm SS carburettors with flat float bowls similar to the 125. The power was 43bhp at 11,600rpm (at the crankshaft), providing the 250 with a top speed of around 135mph (217kmh). Unfortunately the engine was too powerful and too heavy for the scaled-up 125 double cradle frame, and even with Norton forks and Girling shocks the handling was poor. The brakes were Oldani twin leading shoe (220mm and 200mm) but the machine was considerably overweight – a claimed 112 kg (247lb) was plainly optimistic – and suffered from poor acceleration.

The 250 twin was first revealed in February 1960 but when Hailwood flew out for testing it wasn't ready. Later in February both he and Farnè rode it at Modena and were satisfied with the machine. At the end of March it arrived in England and Hailwood gave it a sensational debut at the Hutchinson 100 at Silverstone on 9 April when he won the 250 race. Although Hailwood won again at Brands Hatch and Snetterton, he soon found that while the new Ducati was competitive on the faster circuits it didn't handle well on the shorter tracks. It was sent back to Italy for a new frame, and Hailwood tested this in April, arriving back to win the international race at Silverstone at the end of May. Although the new frame still didn't solve the handling problems, after the Isle of Man Hailwood elected to ride the 250 at the Belgian Grand Prix at Spa and came fourth. He then took the 250 to five consecutive victories on British short circuits before the Ulster Grand Prix, where the 250 appeared with another new frame. Stan Hailwood had commissioned this from Ernie Earles in Birmingham, lengthening the wheelbase from 1,314mm (4ft 3.7in) to 1,372mm (4ft 6in) and lowering and moving the engine further forward. The frame tubing was Reynolds 531. Even though Hailwood came fourth at Ulster he still wasn't overly impressed with the handling, and apart from Snetterton (where he won on the 250 twin), he chose his ageing (1957) Mondial for the rest of the 1960 British season. He did ride the 250 twin early in 1961, winning again at Snetterton, but was disqualified at Silverstone as he was entered on a Mondial.

Both the Hailwood 250s were purchased by John Surtees during 1961. Surtees recognised that the Ducatis were powerful if underdeveloped, and installed the engines in Ken Sprayson Reynolds frames with leading link forks as already built for the Hailwood 350. Initially the Ducatis were for John's younger brother Norman, who raced the 250 several times towards the end of 1961. Before the 1962 season a new frame without a lower right frame tube was produced but Norman had little success with it. John Hartle was set to ride the twin in 1963 but this didn't happen. However, Mike Hailwood gave the 250 one final victory at Mallory Park at the end of March. His final ride on a Ducati until 1977 was at Silverstone in early April 1963, where he rode the Surtees 250 twin to second place behind Redman's Honda.

One of Hailwood's 250 Desmo twins early in 1960. The mechanics on the left are Folesani and Armaroli, with Farnè and Recchia on the right. (Museo Ducati)

THE 350

After a promising season on the 125 Bialbero during 1959 Ken Kavanagh was also interested in a larger capacity twin for the 1960 season. As Stan Hailwood had an exclusivity clause inserted in his contract for the 250, Ken Kavanagh persuaded Taglioni to produce a full 350. Kavanagh signed an agreement in September 1959 for Ducati to supply one 350 Desmo twin for three million lire. However, during November Ducati tried to negate the contract and only reluctantly agreed to supply the machine after legal pressure. According to Kavanagh 'upon hearing about the 350 Stan Hailwood also ordered one and he had more financial clout than I did.' The 350 was largely based on the 250, and with a bore and stroke of 64 x 54mm produced a claimed 48bhp at 11,000rpm (at the rear wheel). The forks on Kavanagh's machine were standard Norton Roadholders that 'were absolutely useless for racing'.

Kavanagh received the 350 in time for the Imola Gold Cup in April, while Hailwood had his by 26 May. In practice Kavanagh found the 350 vibrated badly, and he didn't race it as he crashed the factory 125 Desmo after the sump plug fell out. The 350 then spent a month at the factory before Kavanagh managed to extricate it for the Isle of Man along with mechanic Mario Recchia. There were no spares, and after a rocker broke in practice the machine was sidelined. Kavanagh's next, and final, ride on the 350 was at the Italian Grand Prix at Monza in September. 'The bike was terrible,' says Kavanagh. 'It vibrated and was barely faster than a Manx Norton.' He pulled into the pits and retired. He kept the 350 for a year before selling it to John Surtees.

Hailwood too found the 350 disappointing, electing not to race it at the Isle of Man. The only other time

Kavanagh's final ride on the 350 twin was at Monza in September 1961, but he found the machine extremely disappointing. *(Ken Kavanagh)*

In an effort to improve the handling of the 350, Hailwood's mechanic Jim Adams had a new frame with a leading link front fork built early in 1961. Here Hailwood tests it at Silverstone. *(Mick Woollett)*

he rode the 350 was also at the Italian Grand Prix at Monza. After managing fifth fastest in practice the rear wheel collapsed in the race. Early in 1961 Hailwood's mechanic Jim Adams had a new frame with a leading link Reynolds frame built for the 350, but Hailwood raced it only twice, at Castle Combe. In May he won his heat but the frame broke in the final, and in July the machine expired. John Surtees then purchased the 350 and, with a new Sprayson frame, entered Phil Read in the 1962 Junior TT. The engine failed in practice and the 350s were put aside for good.

Considering the amazing success of the singles it was surprising that Taglioni decided to pursue the path of weight and complexity with the twins. He obviously believed that more horsepower was needed to win Grands Prix but somehow lost direction by creating a design that was excessively complicated. The whole parallel twin experience also showed that Ducati didn't have the resources to produce and develop one-off racing bikes to order. Possibly these projects were accepted because the economic circumstances at the time were so difficult that any commissions were welcome. Unfortunately doubling up the existing successful singles was a recipe for disaster and what was really needed was a completely fresh approach. The 250 and 350 parallel twins were plagued with troubles from fractured crankcases, broken gears, and electrical and ignition problems. They may have been sophisticated designs but their complexity made them problematic, and their power taxed a chassis that was inherited from lower powered and more balanced designs. If nothing else, the parallel twin episode convinced Taglioni of the virtues of light weight, balance, and simplicity, almost to the point of obsession. All later attempts with multi-cylinder racers were half-hearted.

Despite an impressive technical specification, the 125cc four-cylinder Grand Prix racer never lived up to expectations. *(Phil Aynsley)*

THE 125 FOUR

Back in 1958 Taglioni was still convinced of the necessity for a four-cylinder machine for Grand Prix racing and designed a four-cylinder 125. But with the gradual scaling down of the racing operation the project lay dormant until 1964. Then, at the request of their Spanish subsidiary Mototrans, Ducati decided to resurrect the four, but it was already obsolete despite having four-valves per cylinder. The included valve angle was a wide 90°, although Taglioni didn't feel desmodromic valve actuation necessary with such small valves, and normal coil springs were used. The double overhead camshaft 125 used a train of gears on the left side of the engine to drive the camshafts, and with a compression ratio of 12:1 and four 12mm Dell'Orto carburettors, the 34.5 x 34mm engine produced only 23bhp at 14,000rpm. Even with 12 months of development, the power was only increased to 24bhp at 16,000rpm. There was an eight-speed gearbox and the ignition was by battery with four individual 3-volt coils and tiny 8mm spark plugs. The chassis included a conventional double cradle frame, 32mm Ceriani forks, Oldani brakes, and the weight was 85kg (187lb). Development during 1966 saw a new Marelli ignition driven off an idler gear in the camshaft drive and two 6-volt coils. Although Farnè tested it at Modena during 1965, it was obvious that the 125 four would never match the five-cylinder Honda. Rather than racing it, Ducati instead chose to display the four at European Shows during 1966 and 1967. The four then ended in Latvia before being acquired for the Morbidelli collection in Italy.

Although Ducati in Bologna lost interest in the racing four-cylinder, Mototrans in Barcelona produced a 250 four early in 1967. Dubbed the MT250, this was an independent project, designed by Italian engineer Aulo Savelli. It was an orthodox across-the-frame four, with four vertical air-cooled cylinders. The 44.5 x 40mm four had a compression ratio of 10.5:1 and the gear drive to the double overhead camshafts was in the centre of the engine. There was a seven-speed gearbox, dry multi-plate clutch, and four Dell'Orto 15mm carburettors. The claimed power was 50bhp at 14,000rpm. This engine was installed in a duplex frame with 35mm Ceriani forks, Oldani brakes, and Girling shock absorbers, and debuted by Bruno Spaggiari at the Spanish Grand Prix on 30 April 1967. The clutch slip was so bad Spaggiari retired. The MT250 made a brief appearance in practice for the 1968 Spanish Grand Prix but was a dismal failure that was overshadowed by the new desmodromic singles.

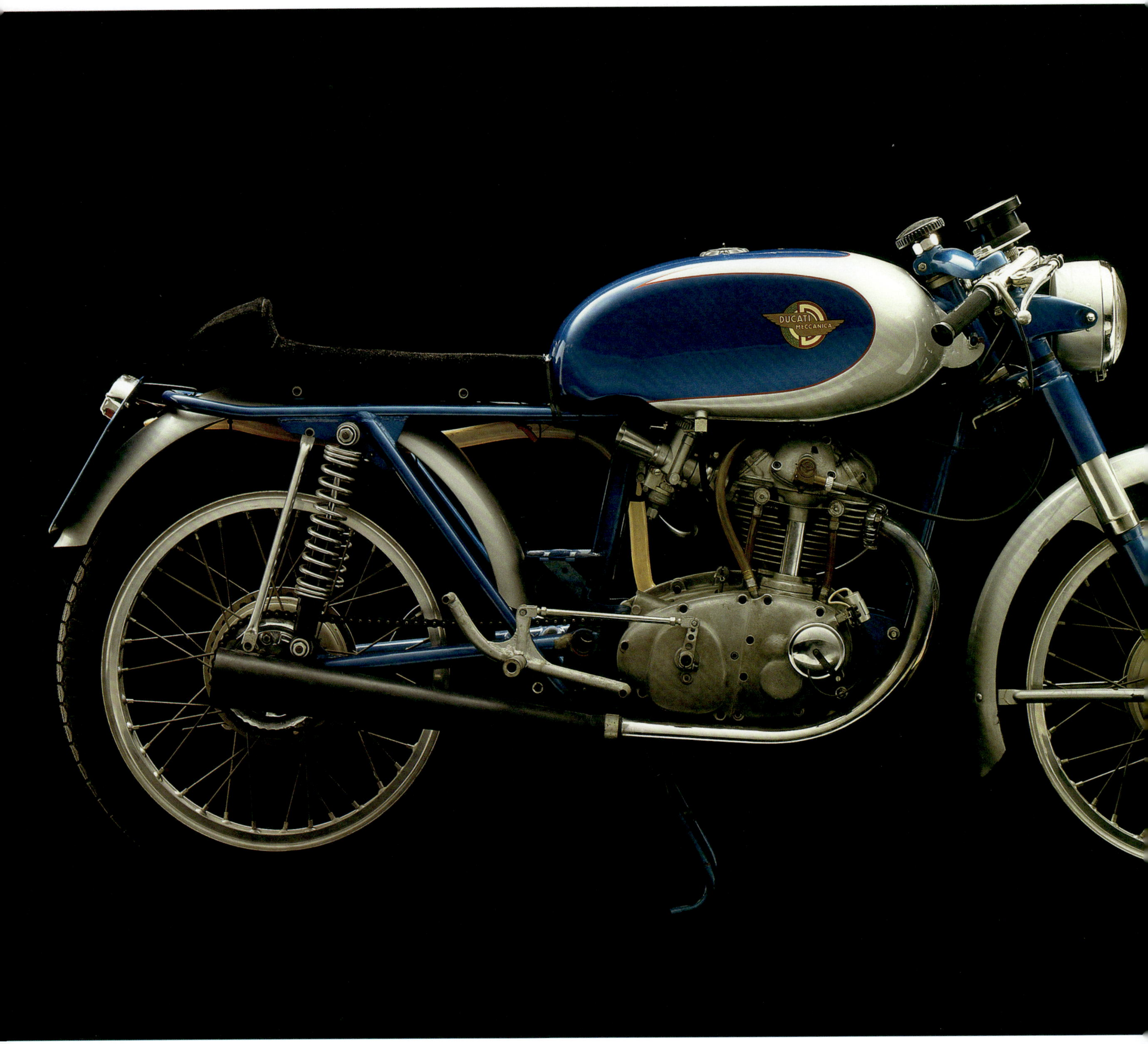
DUCATI
MECCANICA

3 CATALOGUE RACERS

Although the styling differed, the 125 F3 was very similar to the Marianna. *(Roy Kidney)*

As official factory involvement in Grand Prix racing gradually diminished, Ducati looked to the Italian championships to uphold its racing glory. Even by 1957, with the release of the 175 overhead camshaft single cylinder, the emphasis was moving towards development of the road bikes. Some time after 175 production commenced, a new catalogue racer appeared, the Formula 3. Although based on the Marianna which it replaced, this incorporated a number of developments, notably enclosed valve gear. Specifically designed for Formula 3 racing in Italy, its first major success was at Monza in 1958 in the 175 F3 support race for the Nations Grand Prix. Here Franco Villa rode a factory-prepared 175 F3 to win at an average speed of 142.005kmh (88.257mph). With its sand-cast engine this machine was ostensibly a 175 F3, but differed to catalogue F3s in that it featured a production-type sculptured fuel tank, and a smaller (125-type) Amadoro front brake. This result sounded the beginning of a reasonably successful racing career for these beautiful little machines.

THE FORMULA 3

While the desmodromic 125 remained the preserve of factory riders, and the Bialbero the catalogued Grand Prix model, for 1958 the Formula 3 superseded the Marianna as a catalogued production racer. Offered initially as a 125 and 175 (and from 1960 as a 250), the F3 was still largely based on the earlier Marianna, despite the overhead camshaft single entering regular production during 1957. The 125 F3 had Marianna sand-cast crankcases, and apart from the cylinder head with enclosed valve springs was essentially the same motorcycle. The engine dimensions of the 125 were the 55.3 x 52mm of the Marianna, while the 175 was 62 x 57.8mm and the 250 was 74 x 57.8mm.

All F3 engines were special and shared little with the production versions, and the 125, 175, and 250 had different sand-cast crankcases. Inside the engine was a longer crankshaft, supported by two ball bearings in the sand-cast timing case and angular thrust main bearings. The con-rod featured the usual racing style dual strengthening ribs around the big and little end eye and there was a stepped crankpin (32–27mm) with longer (2mm) 3.5mm diameter needle big-end rollers. There were also 20 rollers compared to 18 on the production model. The 125 F3 had a 16mm gudgeon while the 175 and 250 had 18mm gudgeons. The 125 had a 107mm long con-rod while the 175 and 250 shared a longer 125mm con-rod. Like the Marianna there was a four-speed gearbox, and straight-cut primary and bevel gears. Unique to the F3 were mirror image rocker covers, different camshaft covers, and even shorter camshafts than the production versions. As an indication of how unique the F3 was, virtually none of the engine gaskets was interchangeable with a production ohc single.

There were twin oil lines draining from the cylinder head and a tachometer drive from the camshaft bevel drive. Unlike the 125 and 175, the 250 cylinder head also came with bosses for desmodromic closing rocker spindles. Early examples had 8mm rocker pins while the later ones had 10mm pins. The sand-cast F3 cylinder head had the exhaust retained by studs. While the 125 retained the Marianna SS1 20mm carburettor, the 175 F3 had a Dell'Orto SS1 22.5A carburettor (to meet

Right top: Farnè rode a 125 F3 to victory in the 1958 Junior Italian Championship. Here he is at Busto Arsizio in May. *(Museo Ducati)*

Right bottom: Even though the F3 engine looked like the production ohc single, there were few interchangeable parts inside the sand-cast crankcases. *(Ian Falloon)*

Light and reasonably powerful, the 175 was the most successful of the F3s. It also came with twin scoop Amadoro brakes. *(Ian Falloon)*

Italian F3 regulations) or an SS1 27A, and the 250 an SS1 29A. Battery and coil ignition was by a single spark plug, but magneto ignition was optional and each machine came with an individual wiring diagram. The 175 F3 produced 16bhp at 9,000rpm, while the 250 F3 (sold as the Manxman in the UK) made 23bhp at 8,200rpm.

Although patterned after that used on the road versions, the single downtube frame was quite different. Lighter and lower, with a lower steering head, shorter swingarm, and shorter forks, it also varied between models. All these F3s had different dimensions, the 125 with the lowest steering head, shortest 35mm forks, and 18-inch wheels, had identical specifications to the Marianna. The 175 was also a physically small motorcycle with a lower steering head than the 250, although the 175 frame would still accept the 250cc engine. The 175 also had shorter 35mm alloy forks and 18-inch wheels. The 250 F3 was a much larger, and heavier, machine, with special 35mm Marzocchi forks with steel fork legs and 19-inch wheels. It seemed to have been produced for large framed American riders and was arguably overweight.

All F3s had racing specification brakes, with the 125 generally having a Marianna front brake. However, some also had a twin-scoop Amadoro, similar but smaller to that on the 175. The 175 brakes were the same 180mm front and 160mm rear, as most 125 Bialberos, and while the 1961 250 F3 had a 200mm Amadoro front brake, for 1962 there was a 230mm Oldani. Despite their obvious race orientation, many F3s also came with complete street equipment that included a headlight, muffler, tail light, number plate holder, and centre-stand. Although the F3s were genuine factory racing machines they suffered through being too expensive for most privateers and were penalised by the four-speed gearbox. The 125 was essentially a Marianna of 1955 and the 250 was too large and heavy, offering little advantage over a well-prepared Diana. A few 175 F3s were also converted into motocross racers during 1959 and 1960, again with the intention of competing in the US. With a Dell'Orto SSF 25A carburettor the 175 Motocross produced 14bhp at 8,000rpm. However, in the hands

Franco Farnè was involved with every factory racing Ducati for over 40 years. Here he is about to test a 350 SCD at Modena in January 1967, before taking it to Daytona. *(Museo Ducati)*

FRANCO FARNÈ

Of all Ducati's official riders, none have been as loyal to the marque as Franco Farnè. Born on 15 October 1934, Farnè's story is the story of Ducati racing. Both his father and mother worked at the Borgo Panigale plant (although his father wasn't the early Ducati racer Alberto), so when Franco took to motorcycling in 1952 he immediately gravitated to Ducati, first a Cucciolo, followed by a Cruiser scooter. He then acquired a single overhead camshaft Benelli 125 engine, and placing this in a Mondial frame he began racing. It wasn't long before Farnè came to the attention of Eugenio Lolli, who signed him for the first Motogiro d'Italia in 1953 on a Cucciolo. Throughout the 1950s and 1960s Farnè was one of Ducati's leading and most successful riders. Apart from exceptional riding ability, Farnè's other talent was his technical capability, and following the death of Degi Antoni he became Ducati's chief development rider. By 1970 he was primarily a racing technician, and remained at the forefront of Ducati racing machine development until his official retirement in 1996. Even then he was still involved with Ducati until the 2000 season, when he moved to Bimota at the request of his old friend Virginio Ferrari. However, this was short-lived, and by 2001 he was back with the NCR Ducati World Superbike team. Unassuming and spending long hours quietly working behind the scenes, Farnè's life has been spent supervising the preparation of racing Ducatis. Only Franco Farnè can claim an association with every factory racing Ducati from 1953 to the present day.

of Erino Facchini the MVs, Parillas, and Bianchis outclassed the Ducati.

After Villa's success at Monza in 1958 Franco Farnè, accompanied by mechanic Ugo Mastroela, travelled to America early in 1959. With a 125 Desmo and a 175 F3, Farnè's specific purpose was to promote the new range of production ohc singles in the US. He was spectacularly successful and on 5 March rode the 175 to victory in the 250cc event at Daytona, following this with seven more victories throughout the US and Canada before returning to Italy in July.

Farnè continued his winning ways back in Italy, and with the help of Franco Villa provided Ducati with the 175 Junior Italian Constructors' Championship on their 175 F3s. Villa rode for Scuderia Due Torri, or Two Tower (a Bologna trademark) Racing, and had special factory F3s, sometimes with experimental leading axle Ceriani forks with internal springs. Farnè's efforts earned factory representation on a 125 Desmo in the 1960 125 Italian Championship, while Villa went to America with the 175 F3. Villa won four races in the 200 class early in 1960, also campaigning a prototype 250 on occasion. Then he travelled to Barcelona where, teamed with Amedco Balboni, he won the Montjuich 24 Hour race outright on a 175 F3.

Although in Italy the 125 F3 provided Ducati with victories through until 1965, elsewhere the 175 and 200 classes were gradually disappearing in favour of larger capacities. A prototype 250 was produced during 1960 and was immediately successful, Michel Barone winning the French 250cc Championship. In Spain Ricardo Fargas won several races on a Mototrans 250. Then Ducati withdrew from racing altogether at the end of 1960 and there was a period of decline in track success for the next few years. The economic circumstances during this period saw many Italian motorcycle manufacturers disappear as demand for motorcycles in Italy dwindled in the face of cheap cars, and it was only government intervention that allowed Ducati to survive at all. Taglioni, the champion of racing, could do little but grin and bear it, and dream of better times. With no support for racing in Italy, Taglioni turned to Ducati's Spanish connection, Mototrans.

For the 1962 season Spaggiari returned to Ducati, recalling that 'Taglioni and Farnè arranged for me to become an official rider for Mototrans in Spain.' Although Spaggiari had little success that year, Fargas and Enzo Rippa took their Mototrans 250 to victory in the Barcelona 24 Hour race. Farnè also rode in Spain in 1963, and while some national 125 titles (Italy, Canada, Argentina, and Switzerland) were won that year on 125 F3s, this was the first year in nearly a decade that there were no really significant race results. Meanwhile, in the US Ducatis were becoming an increasingly popular choice for racers, both on and off-road. 1961 saw the release not only of the 250 F3, but also of the production 250 Diana. Club racers in America generally liked to modify their machines and enthusiastically adopted the Diana, often in preference to the expensive F3. The Diana was also available with a race kit including a 9:1 forged piston, Dell'Orto 27mm SS1 carburettors, and a megaphone exhaust, making it even more attractive. George Rockett was the only rider consistently sponsored by Berliner with catalogue racers and he rode a 250 F3 to an impressive fourth place in the 1964 US Grand Prix at Daytona behind a works MZ. Already things were looking up for 1964.

Winning the Barcelona 24 Hour race was Ducati's priority in 1964 and for this event Renato Armaroli constructed a special 284cc racer for Spaggiari and Giuseppe Mandolini. Based on the new Mach 1, with a 79mm bore, this didn't have larger crankcases and a double cradle frame as often reported. The frame was the regular single downtube type, but there were racing Ceriani forks and a Grimeca 220mm four leading shoe brake. Spaggiari and Mandolini won the race outright, covering a record 635 laps at an average speed of more than 100kmh (161mph). This success led to the release of the Mach 1/S, ostensibly a Mach 1 with a 250 F3 dual-rib con-rod, magneto ignition, and a 200mm Oldani front brake. Only a few were produced, and with their single downtube frame they were very similar to the production Mach 1. The next development of the racing single, the SC, was more exotic, and the 350 SC debut victory was in the hands of Franco Farnè at Sebring in Florida a week after Daytona in March 1965.

The 1962 250 F3 had a large Oldani front brake, but was still handicapped by a four-speed gearbox. *(Ian Falloon)*

Often confused with the 250 Mach 1/S, the 250 SC shared little with the Mach 1 or Mach 1/S. This is the 1965 250 SC, with a Dell'Orto SS carburettor and Grimeca front brake.
(Ian Falloon)

Attractive and delectable, the 250 SC wasn't as successful as expected but it paved the way for the large crankcase singles.
(Ian Falloon)

THE 250 AND 350 SC

Often erroneously referred to as the Mach 1/S this was actually quite a different machine. The SC (Sport Corsa) was released in 1965, and was available in extremely limited numbers. A second version appeared for 1966. There were specific sand-cast crankcases for the SC, with either 250 or 350 SC and an engine number stamped on the left crankcase near the cylinder. The wider crankcases were designed to accommodate the double cradle frame and there was a close ratio five-speed gearbox. This gearbox was quite different to the Mach 1 and even the later wide-case single, as every gear was wider and the shafts longer. Both the 250 and 350 SC shared the 30/63 straight-cut primary gears. The 74 x 57.8mm 250 had a 125mm long con-rod and a 10.2:1 compression ratio. The 350's dimensions were 76 x 75mm (providing 340cc) and the compression ratio was 10:1. The cylinder head was the sand-cast 250 F3 type, with shorter camshafts (giving 10mm of inlet valve lift) than the Mach 1 and 40 and 36mm valves. Ignition was by twin spark plugs, the 14mm Lodge RL50 supplemented by a 10RL50 on the right. There was a 30-watt alternator and two 6-volt coils in series. Each SC came with its individual wiring diagram and magneto ignition was optional. The carburation for 1965 was by Dell'Orto, an SS1 30 on the 250 and an SS1 32B on the 350.

Apart from the double cradle frame with wider engine mounts that was specific to the SC, there were also special 32mm alloy Marzocchi forks with stepped staunchions (33mm in the lower triple clamp and 31.7mm at the top). The wheels were 19-inch front and rear, and for 1965 the brakes were 230mm Grimeca. The fuel tank was steel in the shape of the Mach 1, and as with the F3 there was full street equipment, including a horn.

Only around 20 250 SCs and half a dozen 350 SCs were built during 1965, and for 1966 there were a few changes. The 250 SC now received an Amal 1³/₁₆-inch 389 monoblock carburettor (the 350 retained the Dell'Orto) and both versions came with 200mm Oldani brakes front and rear. There was a fibreglass tank and humpback solo seat, but the essential dimensions were unchanged. While the wheelbase of 1,320mm (4ft 4in) was moderate, the 250's 115kg (254lb) and the 350's 117kg (258lb) were excessive. Ducati no longer provided an optimistic power figure; instead they claimed an unreasonable top speed of 190kmh (118mph) for the 250 and 200kmh (124mph) for the 350. The SCs were undoubtedly extremely beautiful creations, but as it turned out they were too heavy and the double cradle frame offered little advantage over the standard single downtube type. They weren't spectacularly successful but paved the way for the next racer, the Desmo, debuted by Farnè at Modena on 20 March 1966. This first desmodromic 250 was a modified 250 SC, with the double cradle frame. However, when it became a catalogue racer for 1967 the Desmo was more closely related to the regular production machines.

THE 250 AND 350 SCD

As the 250 F3 cylinder head was already set-up for desmodromic valve gear it was obvious the SC would receive a desmo head at some stage. Seven SCDs (Sport Corsa Desmos), six 250s, and one 350 were entered at Daytona in 1967. One was for Farnè in the Expert Lightweight race, but the desmodromic Ducatis failed the AMA technical inspection as the valve system was considered 'a change in basic design'. As it transpired Ducati received more publicity through not racing against the Yamahas.

These SCDs were quite different to the earlier SC, and were a precursor to the new production wide crankcase singles that appeared at the end of 1967. Rather than special sand-cast crankcases, to save weight and cost, the SCD featured regular die-cast crankcases with a standard ratio five-speed gearbox. This had six selector dogs rather than five, and there were the usual straight-cut primary drive gears and wet multiplate clutch. Both the 250 and 350 SCD were virtually identical, sharing the 135mm con-rod and larger diameter stepped crankpin (30/32mm). The cylinder head was from the 250 F3 and SC, with the exhaust retained by studs and with twin spark plug ignition. There was also an external oil delivery from the cylinder head to the crankcase, just inboard of the timing case. The claimed power for the 250 SCD was 35bhp at

The 250 and 350 SCD featured regular production diecast crankcases and a wet clutch. However, many factory versions, and Reno Leoni's pictured here, often had a dry clutch with sand-cast primary drive cover. *(Ian Falloon)*

Unlike the SC, the SCD had a single downtube frame. There were new, shorter 35mm Marzocchi forks and an Oldani front brake. This is the 1967 250 SCD. *(Mick Woollet)*

11,500rpm, and the 350 SCD 41bhp at 10,500rpm (at the gearbox).

The SCD also had a single downtube frame, constructed of chrome-molybdenum without a loop over the swingarm pivot. The wheels were now 18-inch front and rear, and there were special shorter 35mm Marzocchi forks with alloy fork legs and a steel lower triple clamp. The fork staunchions were no longer stepped and were similar to those on the Scrambler and 450 RT. The brakes were Oldani, and although outlawed at Daytona, ex-patriot Italian Reno Leoni prepared SCDs for Berliner in the US. Leoni maintained a strong connection with Bologna, particularly Taglioni, and in the hands of Rockett and Frank Camillieri his desmos often embarrassed machines twice the capacity. Leoni's 250 ran a 40mm carburettor, and the 350 a 42mm carburettor, and they were initially a match for the 250 Yamaha.

In Italy racing development of the SCD was entrusted to Roberto Gallina and Gilberto Parlotti. Gallina finished second in the 350 race at Modena in March 1967, and continued to achieve some respectable results in early season Italian Riviera street races. These races, known as the Temporada di Primavera (Spring Time Trials), attracted an international entry and were seen as a useful promotional tool. No one expected the desmo singles to beat Hailwood or Agostini, but if Ducati acquitted themselves honourably it would be good publicity. Ducatis have always performed more effectively on home turf and the new Desmo was no exception. Parlotti finished third at Rimini on the 350 behind Pasolini and Hailwood. At San Remo Gallina actually led the 500 race on his 350 Desmo before crashing. Ducati then fielded a factory team at the 1967 Barcelona 24 Hour race, Bruno Spaggiari teaming with Santiago Herrero, but their machines retired.

The SC and SCD may have been the official factory racing machines but in the US the 250cc Diana Mark 3 was the mainstay in the Novice category. Leon Cromer followed a third at Daytona with a runaway win at Laconia. His Mark 3 was fitted with a megaphone, clip-on handlebars, and fairing, but was otherwise surprisingly standard. It was similar in England, where London dealer (and Ducati distributor) Vic Camp's Mach 1s and 350 Sebrings were unexpectedly competitive. At Brands Hatch in July John Williams won the Ecurie Sportive Trophy on a Vic Camp 350.

Ducati made a more determined racing effort in 1968, signing Spaggiari and providing him with desmo singles for three racing classes. Developments over the winter saw an increase in power, the 250 now boasting 36bhp at 11,000rpm with a 36mm Dell'Orto carburettor. The 350 produced 46bhp at 9,500rpm with its Dell'Orto 40mm carburettor, and the clutch was a dry multi-plate type. The brakes were Oldani, a 210mm four leading shoe on the front, and the weight of both models was 111kg (248lb). Also appearing at the opening event at Rimini was the 450 Desmo. Displacing 436cc through an 86 x 75mm bore and stroke, with a 10:1 compression ratio and 42mm carburettor, this produced 50bhp at 9,000rpm.

At Rimini Spaggiari was forced to give in to the new Aermacchi in the 250 event, finishing fourth, but he was a comfortable third in the 350 race. He also made a surprising debut on the 450 after fighting for third but encountering engine trouble on the final lap to finish sixth. Spaggiari continued to achieve respectable results throughout the rest of the season, including third in the 350 race at Cesenatico, and fifth in the Italian 350 Grand Prix at Monza later in the year. He ended third overall in the Italian 350 championship. While the 250 was outclassed by the short-stroke Aermacchi, the 350 Desmo was superior. The 450 spent most of the year in development.

There were also the usual forays into Spain that season. Spaggiari had a 386cc (81 x 75mm) desmo for the Spanish Grand Prix, but retired. At Montjuich it was the British pair of Reg Everett and future Ducati star Paul Smart who rode a Vic Camp Mach 1 to third overall in the 24 Hour race. They also won the 250 class.

For the 1969 season Spaggiari, Gallina, and Parlotti again rode factory 250 and 350 Desmos. There was no 450 racer this year and again the 250 Desmo struggled until Riccione, where Spaggiari led Read's Yamaha and Bryan's Honda before retiring. He made up for this with a fine second at Cesenatico the following weekend on the 250. However, Spaggiari again showed that the 350 Desmo was surprisingly competitive, with a second at Modena, a third at Riccione, and a fourth at Imola. In the Italian 350 Grand Prix he finished sixth. There were also good results elsewhere for Ducati during 1969. Dave Douglas and John McClark won the Baja

BRUNO SPAGGIARI

Although he rode for Ducati, MV, and Benelli, Bruno Spaggiari is best known for his exploits on Ducatis. Spaggiari was born 11 January 1933 in Reggio Emilia. 'I came from a very poor background that I was determined to escape,' he remembers. 'Early on I saw motorcycle racing as my saviour.' Spaggiari's first motorcycle was a Cucciolo, and by 1953 he had graduated to a two-stroke Gitan that he raced at Venzano Casina. His first victory came the following year, by which stage he had graduated to a four-stroke 175 Gitan. He was selected by Ducati to ride a Marianna in the 1955 Motogiro d'Italia and from then on he had a virtually unbroken association with the Bolognese company. His first victory on the Marianna was at Cosenza in September 1955, and in 1956 he consolidated his position as one of the team's leading riders by finishing second to Gandossi in the Milano–Taranto 100cc Sport class.

For Spaggiari '1958 was the magic year. I won the Italian Championship on the 125 Desmo and the Nations Grand Prix at Monza, the first time I had ridden a six-speed desmo.' After Ducati retired from Grand Prix racing Spaggiari signed for MV, partnering Ubbiali, but he was always in the shadow of the World Champion. Only at the Nations Grand Prix did he really challenge Ubbiali, and he still claims he only lost because of team orders. The next year saw Spaggiari on a Benelli but he was back with Ducati again for 1962. The only other glitch in his predominantly Ducati career was during 1964, when MV provided their 1960 125 Bialbero racers for him to win the Italian Championship.

Then it was Ducati all the way, and during 1966 and 1967 he was a privateer with factory support. An official rider again in 1968, Spaggiari remained Ducati's number one for the next few years. Still musing about what might have been if he hadn't run out of fuel at Imola in 1972, Spaggiari retired in 1974 to run his own team with future World Champion Franco Uncini. Following his retirement from motorcycle racing he operated a Fiat car dealership in Modena.

Bruno Spaggiari's career as a works rider for Ducati lasted nearly 20 years. Here the 39-year-old Spaggiari awaits the start of the 1972 Imola 200. (Giovanni Perrone)

In Italy, Spaggiari proved the 350 Desmo was surprisingly competitive and he came third at Rimini in 1968 behind Agostini and Hailwood. (Mick Woollett)

1000 off-road race in Mexico on a modified 350 SSS Scrambler, and at the Isle of Man Alistair Rogers rode a four-year-old Mach 1 to victory in the 250 Production TT at an average speed of 83.79mph (134.82kmh), while Chas Mortimer finished third on a Vic Camp Mark 3.

The 450 Desmo made a reappearance for the 1970 season, now with a claimed 50bhp at 9,000rpm (at the rear wheel). The compression ratio was up to 10.5:1, and the engine was more closely related to the production versions. There was no longer a dry clutch or separate oil drain lines to the timing case. There were also rumours of a four-valve cylinder head but this doesn't appear to have raced. The forks were 35mm racing Ceriani and the front brake a 210mm four leading shoe Fontana. With a reinforced frame and swingarm the 450 weighed 120kg (265lb). Without official factory sanction the machines were entered under the Scuderia Speedy Gonzales team of Farnè, Nepoti, Caracchi, and Librenti. Spaggiari only rode the 450 during 1970 but Parlotti also rode the 250 and 350 Desmos.

The extended period of development on the 450 paid off and Spaggiari was immediately competitive against the singles and twins on the Italian street circuits. He finished fourth at Cesenatico and fifth at Cervia. At Rimini he held second for much of the race, and he also rode brilliantly at Modena and Riccione. Over at the Isle of Man Chas Mortimer gave the Ducati single its second 250 Production TT in 1970, winning on a Vic Camp Mark 3 at 84.87mph (136.56kmh). In the Tuscan Mountain Championship (hill climb racing) the desmo single dominated up until 1974, especially in the hands of future factory Laverda racer Augusto Brettoni.

By 1971 the factory was concentrating on developing the 500 V-twin so the singles were put aside. Spaggiari continued to maintain his line-up of desmo singles, running a racing school during 1971, and the 350s appeared at Silverstone for the John Player International on 13 August 1972. Spaggiari and Ermanno Giuliano entered the Junior event, but there was no longer any future for a four-stroke single in international road racing. Anyway, Ducati was now set on a twin-cylinder path that would ultimately prove even more successful.

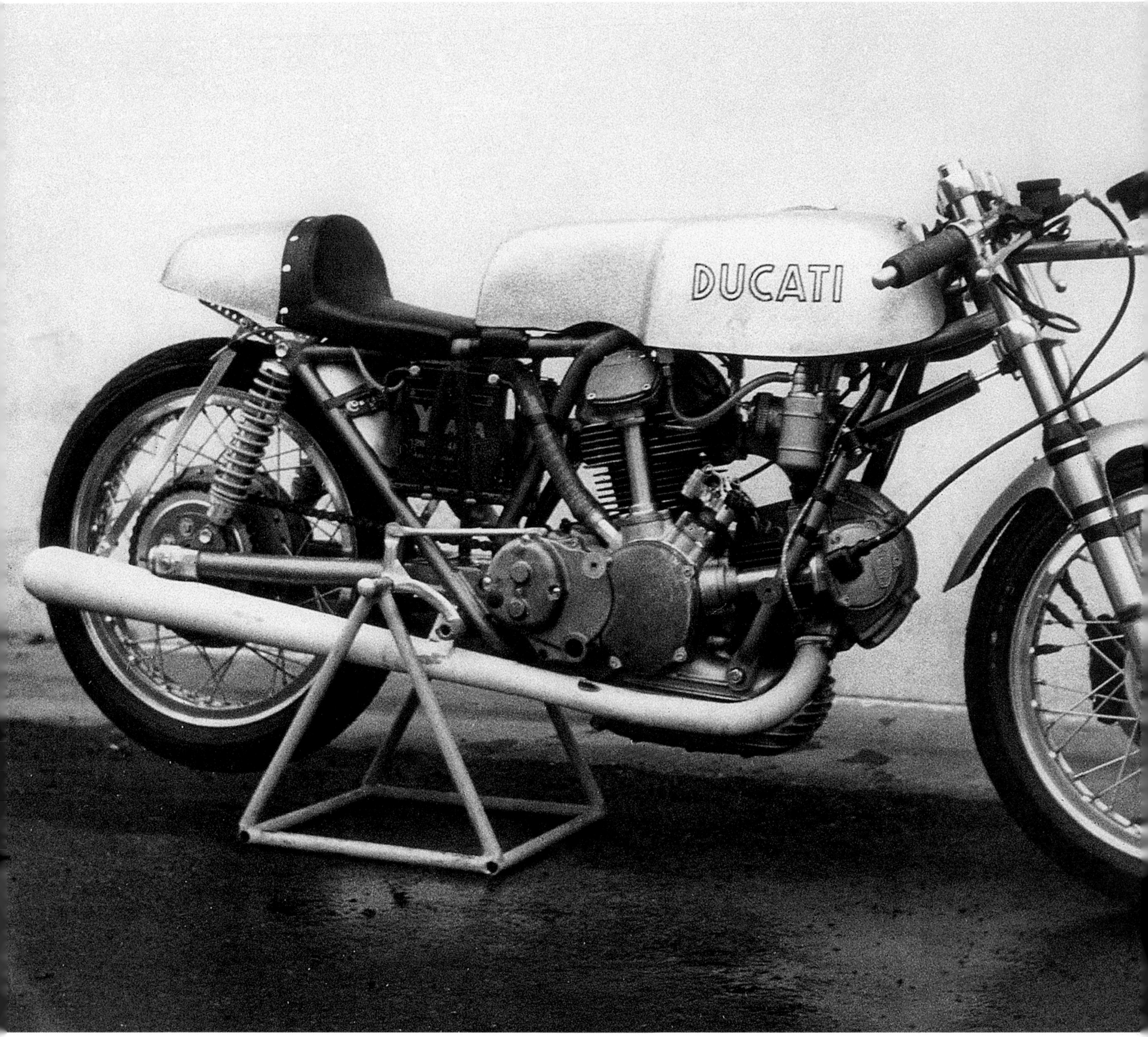
DUCATI

4 PIVOTAL SUCCESS: IMOLA AND DAYTONA

In early 1971 the first 500 Grand Prix racer was unveiled. This featured a Ducati-designed frame and a drum rear brake. (Carlo Perelli)

Although the 1960s were particularly troubled for Ducati, by 1970 things were looking brighter. During 1969 the financial situation became so precarious that the government was called in to supply a direct injection of capital. This resulted in the company coming under direct government control as part of the EFIM (Ente Finanzaria per gli Industrie Metalmeccaniche) group, with a new Director, Arnaldo Milvio, and General Manager, Fredmano Spairani. Not only did Milvio and Spairani come with funding, but they brought with them a passion for racing. Their immediate effect was to sanction the production of a 750cc V-twin, followed by a return to Grand Prix racing.

The 750 twin materialised almost immediately. Taglioni began work on the design in March 1970 and had an engine running by July. By August a prototype was under test, but development stalled following a board meeting in October when it was decided to re-enter 500cc Grands Prix. Taglioni always preferred to work on racing designs and the 500 took immediate precedence over the 750, effectively delaying 750 production for nearly a year. Initially the plan was to build six 500cc V-twin racers to race in the 1971 Italian Championship and some Grands Prix. Two would remain in Italy, with the others going to selected distributors around the world. The official announcement came at a press conference in London in January 1971, where Ducati sent a six-man delegation to announce their intentions to the English-speaking world. Milvio stated: 'The purpose of the 500 is not so much to win races as to prove that the idea of the V-twin is sound, and to promote sales of the sports 750.' Future plans also included a 900, and Milvio talked of subcontracting frame and suspension components so as to facilitate production in time for the 1971 Isle of Man Production TT. As this required a minimum of 100 machines manufactured it was an optimistic expectation, and it was only when the Formula 750 1972 Imola 200, the Daytona of Europe, was announced that Ducati found a suitable category for their new Superbike. In the meantime they persevered with the 500.

THE 500 V-TWIN

True to form Taglioni managed to produce the 500 GP engine very quickly. While the basic layout was similar to the 750, with a 74mm bore and 58mm stroke, the engine was more compact. The crankcases were much narrower to allow the exhaust pipes to tuck in, and as there was no alternator the crankshaft was shorter. The clutch was dry and there was a six-speed gearbox. Ignition was electronic, provided by nearby Ducati Elettrotecnica. Taglioni told the author: 'The 500 still featured an 80° included valve angle and the first version had valve springs as desmodromic valve gear initially provided no appreciable power increase.' With a 10.5:1 compression ratio and Dell'Orto SS1 40mm carburettors the power was 61.2bhp at 11,000rpm. Taglioni also experimented with a four-valve version, but was disappointed with a power output of only 65bhp at 12,000rpm. The set of four-valve cylinder heads was bench tested through until the end of 1972 but the power only rose to 69bhp at 12,500rpm. As the two-valve engine was then producing 71bhp this contributed to Taglioni's suspicion of four-valve cylinder heads. The four-valve heads still featured the wide included valve angle, and twin exhausts for each cylinder.

On British distributor Vic Camp's recommendation, while in England in January 1971 Spairani commissioned Colin Seeley to build a frame for the 500 in order to speed up development. A set of crankcases was despatched and Seeley's brief was to supply two frames along the lines of his successful G50 Matchless version. Built of Reynolds 531 tubing and incorporating an alloy fuel tank with deep knee cutaways, this weighed less than 10kg (22lb) and was finished by mid-February. It was then sent to Italy, but for some reason Ducati didn't use Seeley's frame immediately. Ducati produced their own frame along the lines of the prototype 750 GT, incorporating a swingarm with Seeley-type chain adjusters. Marzocchi provided special 35mm leading axle forks with a single Lockheed front disc brake, and at the rear were Ceriani shock absorbers and a 200mm Fontana double leading shoe drum brake. The wheels were 18-inch front and rear, with 3.00 and 3.25-inch Dunlop tyres. Wheelbase was a moderate 1,430mm (4ft 8in), and the weight 135kg (298lb).

The race debut for the 500 was at Modena on 19 March in the hands of Ermanno Giuliano and Spaggiari, but both retired. Then at Imola on 12 April Giuliano finished second to Agostini, after Spaggiari retired with gearbox failure while holding second place. The next week at Cesenatico Giuliano again finished second, but only after Spaggiari diced with Agostini for the lead until his engine seized. Watching from the sidelines, Phil Read approached Spairani regarding a ride at Silverstone in August.

This must have been the impetus to finally use the Seeley frame, and the revised machine was immediately successful, Gilberto Parlotti giving the 500 its only victory, at Skopia Locka in Yugoslavia on 30 May. Seeley was commissioned to produce five more frames and the Seeley-framed 500, along with factory mechanic Fuzzi Librenti, then went to England, where Vic Camp rider Alan Dunscombe tested it at Snetterton. Marzocchi forks and a Lockheed disc replaced the Seeley forks and drum brake. Read and Spaggiari then tested the 500 at Brands Hatch, both being pleased with the performance and handling.

At the international Silverstone meeting on 22 August, where Hailwood was also to debut the 750, Read got up to third in the 500 race before suffering big-end failure. Spaggiari also fought his way to third before retiring with ignition problems. The Ducatis had impressed everyone with their speed and after the race Spairani optimistically announced: 'We plan to build a batch of 100 500cc racers, and they will be ready by March, in time for the 1972 racing season.' Of course, these didn't materialise. According to Taglioni, 'only five 500s were built.'

There were two 500 twins plus the proven 450 single (75) at Modena in March 1971. From the left are Mazzanti, Giuliano, and Librenti. Farnè sits on Spaggiari's machine, while Spaggiari discusses tactics with Spairani. *(Carlo Perelli)*

Colin Seeley with his prototype 500 frame early in 1971. *(Mick Woollett)*

PIVOTAL SUCCESS: IMOLA AND DAYTONA **55**

Librenti working on the Seeley-framed 500 at Monza in 1971. By now the ignition was battery and coil. *(Carlo Perelli)*

Phil Read on the 500 twin at San Remo in October 1971. He came second to Agostini. *(Museo Ducati)*

Giuliano on the 1972 500 at Modena early in the season. There was new bodywork, but still only a single front disc brake. (Museo Ducati)

Following Silverstone it was back to Italy, where Giuliano and Spaggiari again retired at Pesaro but Read managed fourth in the Italian Grand Prix at Monza on 14 September. Read's average speed was an impressive 114.61mph (184.41kmh). Now running battery and points ignition (the battery strapped to the right side of the engine), Spaggiari was up to second behind Pagani's MV before a broken valve forced his retirement. The final outing for 1971 was the San Remo Grand Prix on 10 October. Although Agostini won easily the Ducatis put up an impressive performance, the three machines of Read, Parlotti, and Giuliano finishing second, third, and fourth. Ducati were well pleased with their first season and looked forward to 1972. However, there was a setback when their intended rider Read signed with MV.

Taglioni also knew that, despite its light weight and excellent handling, the 500 twin would never match the power of the MV. Thus they planned a 500 four, and Ducati's racing emphasis shifted towards Formula 750, although there was still some development on the 500. On 15 March 1972 three 500s were tested at Modena, one with experimental fuel injection and the others with new Dell'Orto PHM 40 carburettors. These now featured a fibreglass 'Imola-style' fuel tank and a rear Lockheed disc brake, and one had a dual disc front end. According to Taglioni, 'With desmodromics the power was up to 69bhp and the engine was safe to 12,500rpm.' The use of titanium also saw the weight down to 127kg (280lb). The fuel injection worked well but was discarded after the FIM declared the system a form of supercharging.

Spaggiari and Giuliano rode the revised 500s at the opening 1972 round at Modena, both retiring, but it wasn't until the Italian Grand Prix at Imola on 21 May (one month after the Imola 200) that the 500 was raced again. Here Smart teamed with Spaggiari once more, with Sergio Baroncini on a third machine. Smart led before being forced into the pits with a loose carburettor. 'That machine was incredibly fast,' Paul told the author, 'almost as fast as the MV, and handled beautifully. It was a real racer.' Spaggiari finished third – at 153.24kmh (95.24mph) – with Smart fourth and Baroncini seventh. At the Yugoslavian Grand Prix at Opatija on 18 June Baroncini finished eighth, and the final official outing for the 500 was at the John Player

The Armaroli 500 twin featured twin overhead camshafts, driven by toothed rubber belts on the left. (Phil Aynsley)

International meeting at Silverstone on 13 August. For this event Ducati took 500s for Smart, Spaggiari, and Giuliano, but outside Italy they never seemed to perform as well. Along with four Imola 750s and a brace of 350s they presented a formidable line up, but this was the end of Ducati's large scale racing involvement for many years to come.

By now the company administration was requiring results to sanction racing and the success in Formula 750 and Endurance saw an end to official 500 development. Taglioni knew the 500 needed more power but as he was involved with the short-stroke 750 Imola racer he engaged former factory mechanic Renato Armaroli to create a double overhead camshaft four-valve belt-drive cylinder head. Armaroli gained his experience working at Tecno with Formula 2 BMW engines and grafted these cylinder heads and belt camshaft drive onto the existing crankcases. The exposed toothed belts were driven from the crankshaft inside the primary gears, so the drive moved from the right side of the engine to the left. Ignition was by a set of contact breakers mounted on the external reduction gear. The front cylinder featured radial finning, and with both Dell'Orto carburettors between the cylinders, and a rear exiting exhaust for the rear cylinder, the power was increased to 74bhp at 12,000rpm. Though Spaggiari appeared on the Armaroli 500 at the opening Italian round at Imola in March 1973 it was obvious the days of four-strokes in 500 Grand Prix racing were over.

THE 750 V-TWIN

Also at the board meeting of October 1970, not only was the development of a 500 V-twin sanctioned, but also that of a Formula 750 racer. Initially development of the 750 was secondary to that of the 500, but by July a racing 750 had been produced and was taken to Silverstone, where Mike Hailwood tested it. In practice for the F750 event on August 22 Hailwood managed sixth fastest, but he decided against riding it as it didn't handle well enough. Apart from the bore and stroke of 80 x 74.4mm this 750 shared little with the 750 GT just entering production, and was essentially a bored and stroked 500 GP machine. It used the 500 crankcases and six-speed gearbox, Dell'Orto 40mm SS1 carburettors, Seeley frame,

Designed by Ricardo, the double overhead camshaft four-valve 350cc triple was another multi-cylinder disaster for Ducati. *(Author's collection)*

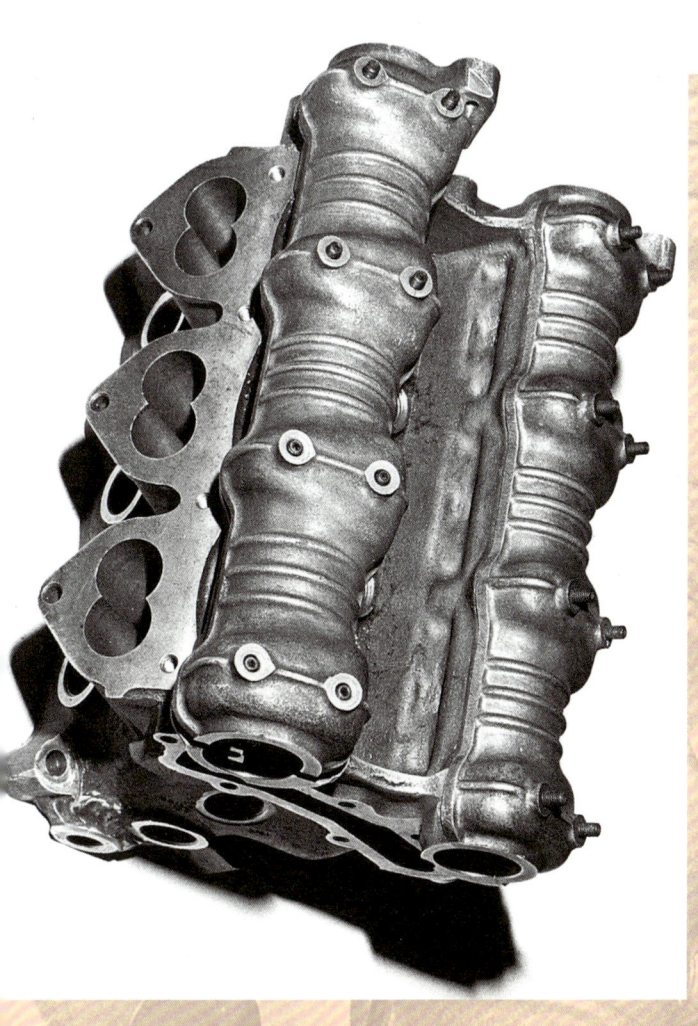

THE 350CC GRAND PRIX TRIPLE

As part of Spairani and Milvio's plan to re-establish Ducati as a racing force the British company Ricardo was commissioned to design a 350cc three-cylinder engine that could beat the then dominant MV. If the 350 was successful they would also sanction a 500 four. While the factory delegation was in England for the Earls Court Motorcycle Show in January 1971 Taglioni outlined their requirements with Martin Ford-Dunne. Ricardo had been involved in some developmental work with the wide-case singles but hadn't any real experience with racing engines since the supercharged BRM Grand Prix car engine. However, according to Ford-Dunne 'the opportunity to get involved in something which turned more than 8,000rpm was too good to miss.' Ducati accepted Ford-Dunne's proposal, but it soon became evident that Taglioni wasn't too interested in the project as he considered it too radical. 'The main concerns to him were water cooling, four valves per cylinder, horizontally split crankcases and fuel injection,' says Ford-Dunne. Taglioni had tried all of these without seeing any advantage, so a new team was set-up headed by Ing. Bruno Tumidei.

The Ricardo design adopted a monoblock casting with the cylinders inclined 30°, and without cylinder head bolt bosses to provide excellent cooling with a high compression ratio. It was very compact, measuring only 234mm (9.2in) across the crankcases. There were double overhead camshafts, 23mm inlet and 21mm exhaust valves with a 40° included valve angle, and flow testing provided the best figures ever seen at Ricardo. Fuel injection was mechanical with continuous feed to the injectors mounted downstream of the 50mm throttles. Cassette-mounted water and oil pumps were gear driven from the crankshaft and there was a removable seven-speed gearbox and dry clutch. Another innovation for the time was the toothed belt drive for the camshafts. With engine dimensions of 60 x 41mm and a 12:1 compression ratio, the maximum power was to be at 17,000rpm with safe revs of 18,250rpm. As electronic ignition was unproven, ignition was battery and coil with three contact breakers driven off the end of one of the camshafts.

While the design layouts were done at Ricardo, the details were drawn in Bologna, with most of the manufacture in Italy. Bearings, valves, springs, timing belts, and fuel injection were obtained in England and Ricardo built the first engine by the middle of 1971. However, there were many problems. The poor quality castings (apparently made by Ferrari) leaked oil and water, but once these problems were overcome there was serious combustion delay. According to Ford-Dunne, '70° of ignition advance was required at 14,500rpm, but we could not obtain any more. The problem was that airflow was achieved at the expense of turbulence.' With only a disappointing 50bhp, carburettors replaced the injection system, but it was now becoming difficult to obtain updated components. Tumidei was forced to do the machining overnight on the new CNC machines because these were engaged on the new 750 twin during the day. Ducati then lost interest in the project and it was scrapped following a meeting between Ducati and Ricardo in August 1972. After this Tumidei worked on the ill-fated parallel twin before going to work at a bottle making plant. It may have been a disaster, but Ford-Dunne recounts that 'the 350cc engine sounded superb, the six individual exhausts giving out a really pleasant wailing noise.'

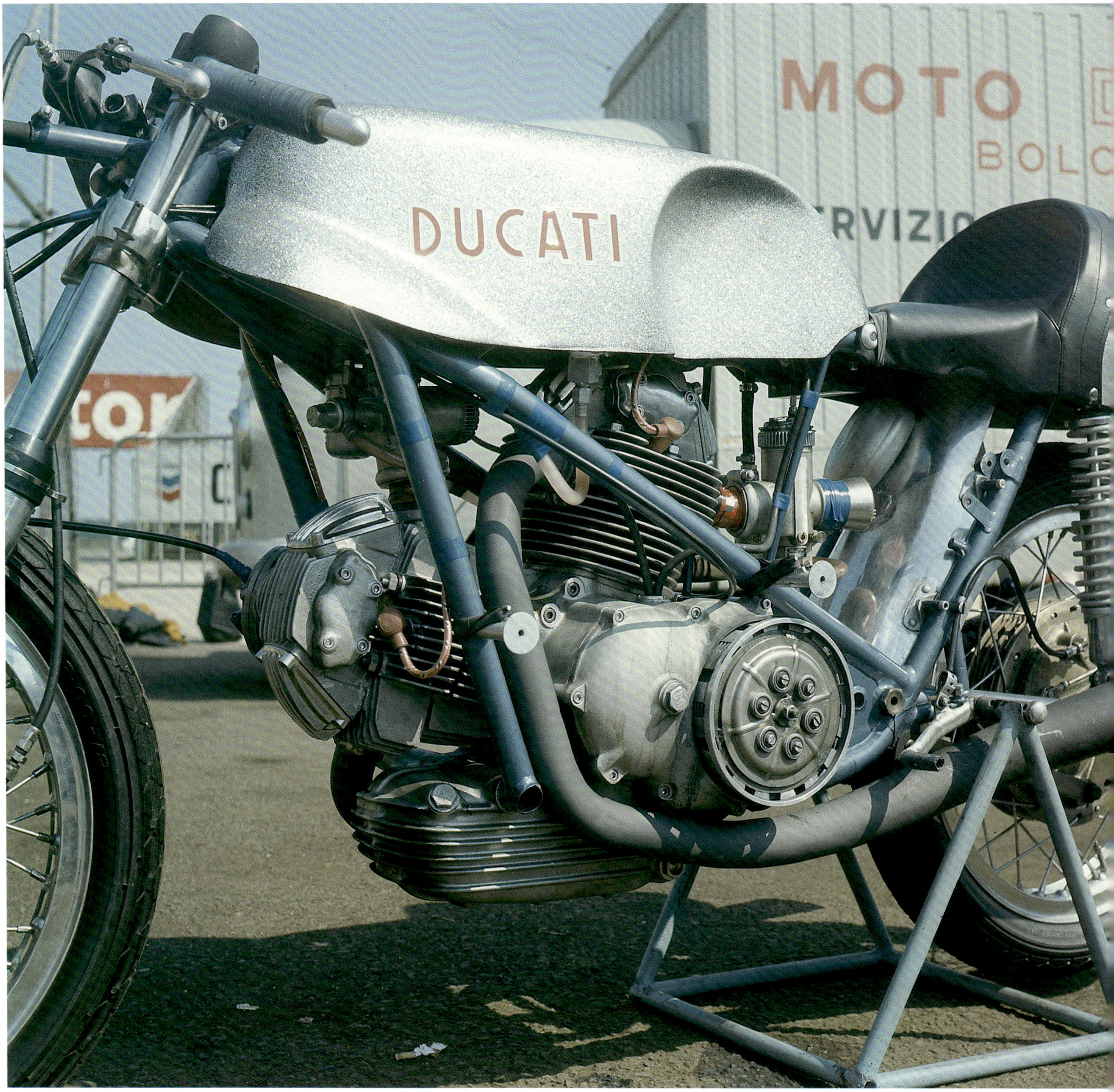
MOTO
BOLC
DUCATI
RVIZIO

and single Lockheed front disc brake. Weighing 163kg (359lb), making 75bhp and revving to 11,500rpm, this first desmodromic 750 taxed the frame and brakes to the limit. Giuliano rode it a few more times in Italy, but when it came to creating the next F750 racer Taglioni turned to his own 750 GT as a basis.

With the announcement of the Imola 200 'Daytona of Europe' to be held on 23 April 1972, Spairani instructed Taglioni to mount a full-scale attempt at winning the race. Not only was this in Ducati's backyard, but the organisation under Dott. Francesco Costa was spending a vast amount on publicity. Thus, to assess the competition, Taglioni travelled to Daytona in March 1972, coming away particularly impressed by the speed of the Yamahas – they went so fast he couldn't read the numbers; but knowing that the 350 Yamahas couldn't race at Imola Taglioni reasoned he could build a balanced machine particularly suited to the Imola circuit. On his return from Daytona he took ten production 750 frames and the race department began building a batch of Formula 750 racers. It was originally intended to build ten machines for six riders. However, as the deals with two riders fell through it is unlikely that ten were constructed as reported in the press at the time. Although both Fabio Taglioni and Bruno Spaggiari told the author that six 1972 750 Imola racers were produced, there were definitely seven in the specially constructed glass-sided transporter at Imola. Franco Farnè indicated to the author that one also remained at the factory as a backup, so possibly eight machines were constructed in all.

Spairani was determined to hire a top rider to head a line-up of six entries. He approached Jarno Saarinen, Renzo Pasolini, and Barry Sheene. In February Sheene agreed (and was listed in the programme on number 18), but didn't race as he couldn't come to an agreement over the fee. Like other top riders he also didn't believe

Opposite: The first 750 racer was based on the 500. It featured a dry clutch, Dell'Orto SS1 carburettors, and the Seeley frame. (Mick Woollett)

Left: Hailwood testing the 750 at Silverstone in August 1971. (Mick Woollett)

Alan Dunscombe rode one of the factory Imola 750s, although his machine had Dunlop TT100 tyres rather than the racing KR83/84 of Smart and Spaggiari. Like Smart, Dunscombe also had lower footpegs. *(Giovanni Perrone)*

the Ducati would be competitive. Already signed were Bruno Spaggiari (on number 9), Ermanno Giuliano (45), Vic Camp's rider Alan Dunscombe (39), and Gilberto Parlotti (24), although he too didn't race. Needing another top rider, Camp suggested Spairani approach Paul Smart, then racing for Team Hansen in America. Paul's wife Maggie accepted the invitation in Paul's absence and Smart initially wasn't too impressed. But Spairani was paying good money, and after a Triumph ride fell through Smart was soon down in the programme on Ducati number 16, listed just ahead of his brother-in-law Barry Sheene. After funding his own way to Imola on a privateer Triumph, Percy Tait was later offered Sheene's machine but declined. He probably regretted this decision but would ride the 750 at Mosport in Canada in July.

The first Imola race bike was completed in time for a Modena test by Spaggiari on 6 April in preparation for the first official test session on the 19th, only four days before the race. Here five machines were available, Smart, Dunscombe, and Giuliano riding them for the first time. Smart came away impressed and all was ready for official practice at Imola on Friday.

Although the racing desmodromic 750s looked surprisingly standard they were highly developed factory racers sharing little with the production 750. The frames may have started as production items but were considerably modified to accept the large fibreglass fuel tank and provide a suitable racing riding position. They did retain the 29° steering head angle but after the 19 April test each rider was able to tailor the machine to suit himself. Thus Smart (and Dunscombe) had the footpegs repositioned lower and a hydraulic steering damper installed. The forks were machined leading axle Marzocchi, providing around 100mm (3.9in) of travel, with standard length 305mm (12in) Ceriani shock absorbers. Many 750 GT parts were modified and adapted for the racer, such as the front 278mm Lockheed discs, with a rear 230mm disc, and 18-inch WM3 Borrani wheels front and rear. As there were only left-side Lockheed calipers in stock for the 750 GT three left-side calipers were adapted for the racers.

The engines too may have ostensibly looked reasonably standard but Taglioni took early production (pre-engine number 750404) 750 sand-cast engine cases rather than the die-cast type used at that time. These were heavier, with an extra sump bolt, but were undoubtedly stronger. Inside was a crankshaft incorporating 50gm lighter solid billet con-rods with strengthening ribs, higher ratio straight-cut primary gears (31/75), and a close ratio five-speed gearbox. To reduce reciprocating weight there was no flywheel or alternator. There were higher compression (10:1) 80mm pistons and desmodromic cylinder heads. The valve sizes were standard 40mm and 36mm, the desmodromic camshafts supposedly provided 13mm of inlet valve lift, and the engine was safe to 9,200rpm. The total loss points ignition system featured twin spark plugs per cylinder, the additional 10mm Lodge spark plug allowing ignition advance to be cut back to 34° before top dead centre. After his experience with electronic ignition on the 500 during 1971 Taglioni wasn't prepared to risk it at Imola. He was also worried about heat build up and installed an oil cooler in the front of the fairing to cool oil to the cylinder heads, also mounting the ignition condensers on the front frame downtubes, away from the heat of the engine. With Dell'Orto PHM 40 concentric carburettors the claimed power was 84bhp at 8,800rpm at the rear wheel. At 7,000rpm the engine was said to make 70bhp. However, just as it is with factory Ducati racing engines today, no one is prepared to say what was really inside those Imola 750s to make them so fast, and as Paul Smart said to the author, 'one of my two bikes was much faster than the other. The fast bike won the race and even later in England that particular engine was more powerful.'

Although the Imola 750 engines looked like those of the production 750 GT, these were real racing motors. This is Spaggiari's machine. Evident are the higher footpegs, and dual ignition.
(Author's Collection)

In many respects the Imola machines were designed for one race only. Knowing there was only one tight right hand corner at Imola (the Aqua Minerale), the kick-start was removed and a close-fitting exhaust pipe installed on the right. The left pipe was high rise, and as Imola was a high-speed circuit the long wheelbase of 1,530mm (5ft 0.2in) wasn't considered detrimental. The dry weight was 178kg (392lb), and despite the rather non-aerodynamic fairing they were reputed to pull the tallest available gearing, giving around 272kmh (169mph).

On race day for the '200 Miglia Shell di Imola' at 5.017km (3.118-mile) Autodromo 'Dino Ferrari' Imola, 70,000 spectators crammed in to see who would win the total prize money of Lire 35,000,000, at that time a world-record. Not only were there four factory Ducatis, but MV Agusta provided machines for Giacomo Agostini and Alberto Pagani, and Moto Guzzi had official entries for Guido Mandracci and Jack Findlay. Then there were the factory John Player Nortons of Phil Read, Peter Williams, and Tony Rutter, the BSA of John Cooper, and the Triumphs of Ray Pickrell and Tony Jeffries. Completing an impressive array of factory machinery were the 750 Hondas of Bill Smith, John Williams, Silvio Grassetti, and Luigi Anelli, and the BMWs of Helmut Dahne and Hans-Otto Butenuth. There were also strong contenders in Daytona-winner Dave Emde, Walter Villa, Ron Grant, and the Kawasakis of Cliff Carr and Dave Simmonds. It was one of the most competitive fields ever in F750.

Spaggiari set the fastest time in practice on the Friday, and along with Smart was fastest again on the Saturday. They repeated this performance on race day, the two silver Ducatis following Agostini for four laps before Smart took the lead. Although he lost first gear early in the race Smart wasn't handicapped and comfortably held first for most of the race. Agostini retired on lap 41 and Spaggiari then overtook Smart on lap 56 before Smart regained it two laps from the end after Spaggiari ran wide on one of the faster corners. Spairani had instructed his two leading riders not to dice for the lead until the final five laps. Both machines were now low on fuel and misfiring, and Smart crossed the line four seconds ahead of Spaggiari, who was only running on one cylinder. The Ducatis proved so dominant that Villa in third was a further 25 seconds behind. Smart's race average was 157.353kmh (97.796mph) and he shared the fastest lap of 161.116kmh (100.134mph) with Spaggiari and Agostini. Giuliano retired and Dunscombe was the only rider to crash, breaking a right collarbone, while in ninth position. It was Smart's 29th birthday and the biggest victory of his career.

Imola 1972 was the most significant victory yet in Ducati's history and amidst the post-race euphoria Spairani was intent on maximising publicity. Smart was presented with his race-winning machine; Ron Angel, the Victoria (Australia) distributor, negotiated the purchase of Spaggiari's racer; and production Desmo race replicas were promised. As part of the publicity the Imola racers were also campaigned in selected events around the world. Gilberto Parlotti was lent one (fitted with road equipment) to learn the Isle of Man circuit, and at the beginning of July four Imola 750s were sent to Mosport for the Canadian Grand Prix. Richard White, Spaggiari, and Percy Tait raced them, Tait finishing third. According to Tait, Spaggiari's machine was clearly the fastest so he swapped the numbers over while no one was watching. In England Paul Smart campaigned his Imola race winner with moderate success. 'Although we had an 860 to test at Brands Hatch the original 750 was still faster,' says Smart. 'Even after it threw a rod and the crankcases were repaired it was the fastest.' He won the F750 race at Hutchinson 100 and was joined by Spaggiari, Giuliano, and Dunscombe at Silverstone on 13 August. Spaggiari finished sixth in the F750 race and Smart fourth in the 1,000cc event. Smart's final race in England was at Snetterton for the Race of Aces, where he retired. His machine, probably the most famous of all Ducati racers, then went on display in his motorcycle shop in Paddock Wood for many years. Smart's final 1972 outing on an Imola 750 was in October, when he flew out to race a factory-prepared machine in the Greek Grand Prix at Corfu, winning easily. To this day he doesn't even know why he raced there: 'It was barely a race track and there was absolutely no competition,' he says. Following this race one of the 1972 racers was sent to South Africa. Ridden by Errol James in the international summer series, James finished fifth in the South African TT. Two more of the racers ended up in Canada, and one in Germany. But already Taglioni was more interested in developing a new machine for 1973.

Opposite: Smart led for most of the race, and won the 1972 Imola 200 after nearly running out of fuel on the final lap. (Mick Woollett)

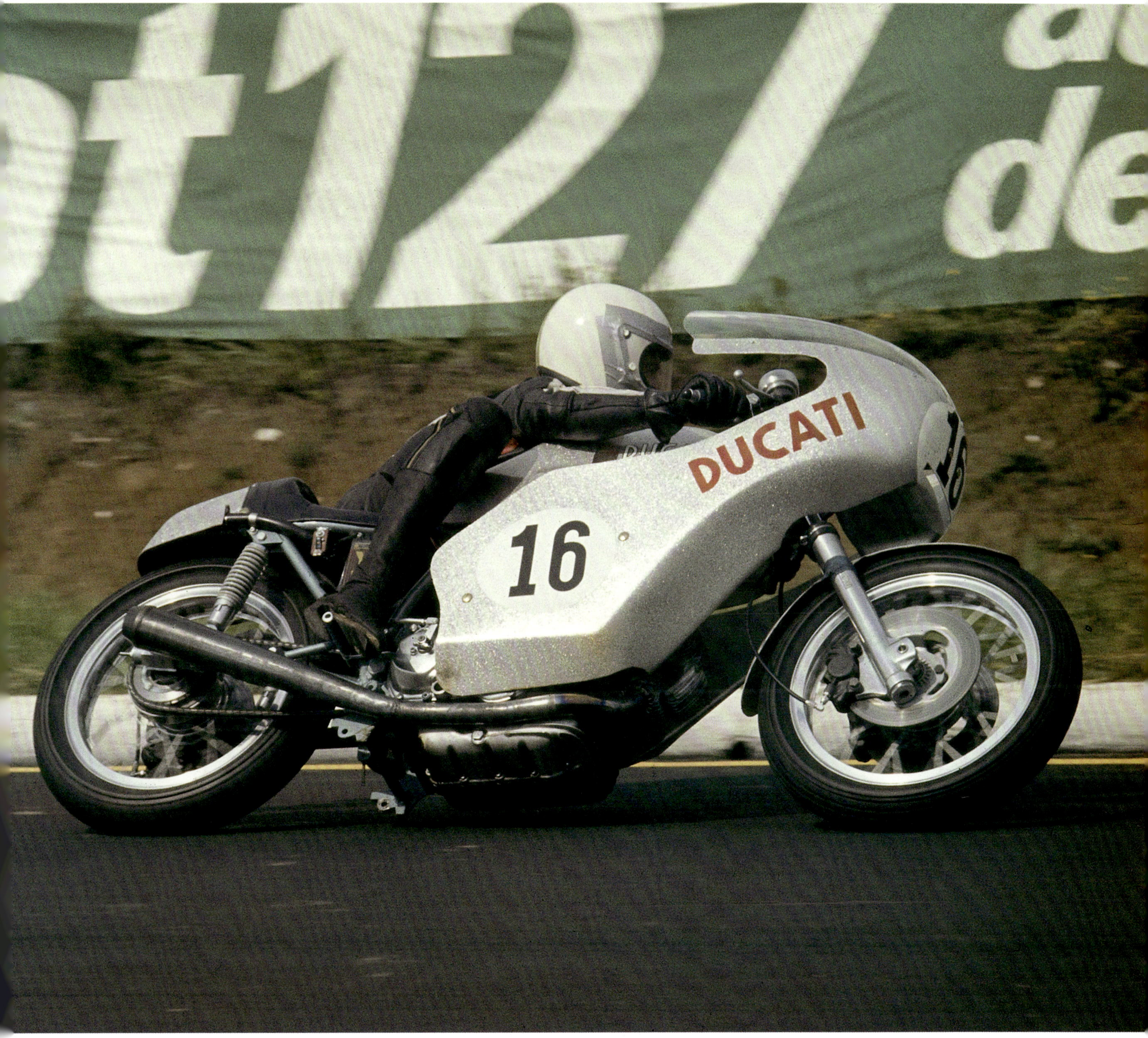
DUCATI
16

Spaggiari, Taglioni (behind), Farnè, and Smart on the victory rostrum after the 1972 Imola 200.
(Mick Woollett)

PAUL SMART

Although he only raced Ducatis a few times, the victory at Imola in 1972 has made Paul Smart one of Ducati's legendary riders. Smart was born in Eynsforsd, Kent, on 23 April 1943, and began racing motorcycles in 1964 on a 125 Bultaco. Smart is often credited with creating the 'hanging off' style, a feature that undoubtedly helped with the long wheelbase Ducati. As Smart says, 'I was handicapped in my café racing days by having a BSA Shooting Star when all my mates had Triumphs. The only way I could keep up with them was to scratch like mad and to stop it grounding by hanging off.' He then went road racing, making his mark by finishing second in the 1967 Production TT on a Norton 750, then switching to 250 and 350cc Grand Prix Yamahas. One of the most adaptable road racers, he had a succession of Grand Prix podium finishes during 1970, as well as winning the Bol d'Or 24 Hour race on a Triumph. This saw him on a factory Triumph triple for 1971, bursting onto the US scene when he qualified fastest at Daytona and led the event until his Triumph melted a piston ten laps from the chequered flag.

For 1972 he signed with Bob Hansen to race Kawasaki H2-Rs in the US, also jetting back to England to race in several meetings. It was while in England that he commissioned Colin Seeley to build a frame for the evil-handling H2-R. With this frame Smart won the world's richest road race at Ontario, California, capping off a highly successful year. He was on Suzukis for 1973 and his last race on a Ducati was at Imola in 1975. Still on crutches after breaking both thighs in a crash, he pulled in while in eighth place after the engine lost 200/300rpm. 'Farnè sent me out again, and heeled over in second gear on the overrun it seized,' says Smart. It may have been an inglorious finale but fortunately Maggie Smart's acceptance of Spairani's offer back in 1972 was, in her words, 'the best decision I ever made.'

Immediately after the Imola victory, Fabio Taglioni embarked on developing a new racer for 1973. Although he appreciated the success of the production-based 1972 machine he knew that the next generation racer must be lighter, more powerful, and have a shorter wheelbase. Remaining committed to the 90° V-twin, Taglioni set about creating a more compact engine. He also updated the cylinder head to provide a narrower 60° included valve angle allowing a higher compression ratio with a flat-topped piston, without twin spark plug ignition.

With a ready supply of 86mm racing pistons from 450s available, Taglioni chose a shorter, 64.5mm stroke to attain 750cc. Thus, apart from production-based crankcases (again based on an early sand-cast 750 GT), the entire engine was created from scratch. This not only meant special sand-cast cylinder head castings, but shorter barrels and bevel gear drive shafts. The 60° cylinder heads also required one-off (12mm lift) camshafts and rockers for the 42 and 38mm valves. With closer valve interference due to the 60° heads higher valve lift wasn't possible. Even a special magnesium ignition points housing needed to be fabricated to clear the carburettor.

Along with the shorter stroke came shorter milled 750 SS-style con-rods. With an eye-to-eye length of 130mm (5.12in) they were 20mm (0.79in) shorter than before, resulting in an engine 25mm (0.98in) shorter and lower. The gudgeon was also reduced 2mm to 20mm. There was the usual pressed-up roller bearing crankshaft, no alternator or flywheel, and total loss points ignition. Still with higher ratio straight-cut primary gears (33/71) and a special drilled close ratio gearbox, the main development was a dry clutch, requiring a special long step mainshaft.

Although Taglioni completed the engine drawings by May 1972, and had the unfinished head castings by July, political activities at the factory and strikes saw all development halted until February 1973. After enthusiastically supporting racing prior to Imola, Spairani now considered the job done and wouldn't sanction similar involvement. Then in a surprise move Spairani was ousted and replaced by Ing. DeEccher from Aermacchi. DeEccher would later prove Taglioni's nemesis but initially allowed the development of the new 750 racer to continue. Unfortunately strikes pertaining to the renewal

Above: Although it used production crankcases, the short-stroke 1973 engine shared few other components and was specifically designed for racing. (Phil Aynsley/Two Wheels)

Left: As with all Ducati factory racing engines, the crankshaft of the 1973 750 was heavily machined, and the con-rods featured dual strengthening ribs. (Phil Aynsley/Two Wheels)

The line-up of three 750s at Imola in 1973. Taglioni is behind, with Recchia tending Spaggiari's machine (84), and Mazzanti, Kneubuhler's (86). *(Author's Collection)*

Kneubuhler set the fastest lap in the first leg, but crashed. *(Mick Woollett)*

of the metalworkers' contracts almost saw an end to the project and these weren't resolved until a month before the 1973 Imola race. Another setback occurred when Farnè and Massimo Nepoti (son of mechanic Giorgio Nepoti who founded NCR) collided on the Bologna Tangenziale while testing 750s. Nepoti was killed and Farnè badly injured. Still, by March 1973 Taglioni had not only completed the engine, but had managed to design a new shorter frame with eccentric chain adjustment at the swingarm pivot and a choice of three rear axle positions to alter the wheelbase. Built by frame specialists Daspa in chrome-molybdenum, this resulted in a wheelbase of only 1,420mm (4ft 7.9in) with the axle in the shortest location. A unique feature of racing Ducati engines was that the date of assembly was often inscribed underneath the piston crown, with 22 February 1973 on one of these engines.

Two weeks before Imola Spaggiari tested the bike at Modena. With Ceriani shock absorbers and the earlier leading-axle Marzocchi forks Spaggiari complained of instability. He then tried a makeshift set-up comprising a set of new centre-axle Marzocchi forks, retaining the earlier flat triple clamps. Stability reappeared, and this fork set-up (with forward-mounted Scarab calipers) eventually featured on the production 1974 750 Super Sport. While there were problems getting the engine to rev past 9,500rpm in Ducati's reverberant dyno room, out on the track the engine pulled cleanly beyond 10,400rpm. Not only was the bike much more nimble, it was considerably lighter at 148kg (326lb), and more powerful with around 90bhp at 10,000rpm. In testing Spaggiari managed to better Agostini's outright lap record set on a 500cc MV triple so everything looked good for Imola. This year, though, there were only the resources to build three machines, with the final one completed on the Thursday before the race. Spaggiari again rode, joined by British star Mick Grant and rising Swiss ace Bruno Kneubuhler.

The 1973 Imola 200 was even bigger than in 1972. Even without the draw card of Agostini more than 100,000 spectators turned up on 15 April for the race, run in two 100-mile (160km) legs. This played into the hands of Saarinen and his two-stroke Yamaha, who took out both races. However, the Ducatis put in an impressive showing considering their lack of race development. In the first leg, Kneubuhler was lying second

During 1973 the short-stroke 750s were kitted out with a headlight, larger fuel tank, and rear brake scoop for endurance racing. *(Museo Ducati)*

Spaggiari again raced the short-stroke 750 at Imola in 1974, but this was his final ride. *(Mick Woollett)*

Smart's final Ducati ride was also on the 750 at Imola. For the 1975 race he was entered under Spaggiari's banner. *(Mick Woollett)*

70 DUCATI RACERS

and closing on Saarinen before he was knocked by a slower rider and crashed, breaking a thumb. Kneubuhler did set the fastest lap, though, at 165.147kmh (102.639mph). Grant burnt out his clutch on the start line but Spaggiari finished second. In the second race Spaggiari came third, taking second overall, and in both races his average speed was more than 3kmh (1.9mph) up on the race winning speed of 1972. The evergreen Spaggiari (then 40 years old) may have been beaten by the genius of Saarinen but there were a host of illustrious names behind him, including Kel Carruthers, Cal Rayborn, Walter Villa, and Teuvo Lansivuori. Considering the machines were hastily prepared, Spaggiari's performance was impressive.

After Imola the 750s were converted into endurance racers, with headlights and Dunlop TT100 tyres, with the intention of running them in the Bol d'Or. However, nothing eventuated in endurance racing and following the 1973 Milan Show Keith Harte in Canada managed to purchase the Spaggiari machine. The other two were kept for Spaggiari to race in the 1974 Imola 200, basically unchanged but for Lockheed front disc brakes. Spaggiari managed eighth in the first leg before retiring in the second. One of these machines (Kneubuhler's from 1973) went to Spain, where Jose Maria Mallol rode it in the Spanish F750 series, which he won in 1976. Coburn and Hughes also managed to borrow the other 750 for some British races during 1974. Doug Lunn rode it at the Isle of Man and Percy Tait at Silverstone, before it returned to Italy. 'For the 1975 Imola 200 Taglioni wanted Paul Smart to ride, but it was entered under my banner,' says Spaggiari. It was unfortunate that the 1973 Imola 750s coincided with active discouragement of racing by Ducati's management, and the non-competitiveness of four-strokes in F750. Taglioni therefore considered the 1973 Imola racers developmental machines for the next generation, the Pantah, but they were amongst the finest of all Ducati's racers.

While Spaggiari retired from active competition in 1974 he continued to sponsor the 750 SS of future 500cc World Champion Franco Uncini during 1975 in the Italian Championship. Uncini won six 750 races that year, and even during 1976 the 750 SS was a strong competitor in the Italian Championship in the hands of Carlo Saltarelli. But it was on the other side of the Atlantic that the 750 SS would achieve its next important victory.

THE CALIFORNIA HOT ROD

While the Imola 200 victory of 1972 was pivotal to Ducati's success and image in Europe, in the United States the most important race was still Daytona. Because Formula 750 became the preserve of two-strokes after 1972 the Daytona 200-mile race wasn't an event particularly suited to the Ducati 750 twin. This changed with the advent of the Superbike racing class, and on 11 March 1977 *Cycle* magazine editor Cook Neilson raced across the finish line to win the Daytona Superbike race. It was Ducati's most significant victory ever in America. Even with the incredible success of the Desmoquattro in World Superbike, Superbike victory at Daytona has since eluded Ducati.

The most impressive aspect of the victory was that it came without factory support and was undertaken by a pair of journalists rather than professional racers and tuners. While Neilson rode, *Cycle's* executive editor Phil Schilling wrenched. The development of their 750 SS was a broad, collaborative exercise. That effort drew heavily on specialists from the California hot-rod culture, their expertise and technology. The products from this local talent pool often proved superior to official factory parts, both through the front and back door.

When Neilson decided to go production-racing California-style in 1973, the starting point was his own Ducati 750 GT. Neilson's testing for *Cycle* magazine persuaded him that next to its class competitors the Ducati was easier to get into corners, had more ground clearance, and was simply more pleasant to ride fast. His 750 GT soon had high compression pistons, flowed cylinder heads, special valves, and aftermarket camshafts, and Neilson won three club events that year. Very late in 1973 a pre-production 750 SS arrived at *Cycle*, and with this, backstopped by a production 1974 750 SS, Neilson moved into the new American Motorcyclist Association large-displacement production class for 1974. Not fully developed, the Desmo twin was outpaced by the 900cc Kawasakis and BMWs. A brief but unsuccessful experiment resulted in a home-built 926cc Desmo that became unnecessary to pursue.

The establishment of a 750cc production racing

class in 1975 suited both Neilson and the pre-production 750 SS, and they proved invincible against other 750s. The bike was nicknamed 'Overdog' (antonym of 'Underdog'), and it was a genuine 140mph (225kmh) twin running standard carburettors and mufflers. Production rules allowed chassis modifications and these included longer S&W shocks, plasma-sprayed aluminium brake discs, and a WM6 (3.5-inch) rear rim. The cylinder heads were flowed by Jerry Branch, who had worked on Neilson's earlier drag bikes, and Jeff Bratton prepared the stock crankshaft, but it was the use of a Goodyear slick tyre at Riverside that provided the 750 SS with its biggest advantage. The superior Ducati chassis didn't flex as much as those of the Kawasakis and BMWs and allowed the full utilisation of the higher grip slick tyres. Neilson won the Open Production race, beating Reg Pridmore's distributor-sponsored BMW for the first time.

By the end of 1975 Neilson's 750 SS was almost as fast as the open class Kawasakis, and when the AMA rewrote its production-racing rules again for 1976, Neilson and Schilling decided to go for more displacement. The new rules provided for a maximum of 1,000cc, standard carburettor and muffler bodies, and a standard chassis, although strengthening was allowed. The bikes also had to have a working headlamp and tail light. With the factory unable or unwilling to supply replacement cylinder heads Neilson and Schilling decided to go down the hot-rod route, and so 'Overdog' became 'The California Hot Rod'.

Calculations by Jerry Branch indicated the standard cylinder heads could flow more, but not enough to make a 1,000cc engine viable. About 900cc was the maximum displacement airflow would permit, and without access to alternative desmodromic camshafts outside the regular 'Imola' variety it was deemed prudent not to stray too far from the 750 capacity for which the camshaft was designed. As ring seal was a problem on the earlier big-bore Ducati, Neilson and Schilling decided to use proven components from the Yamaha XT500 single and have American Venolia pistons made to suit with lightened Toyota gudgeon pins. Thus the chosen bore was 87mm, giving 883cc. Branch reworked the cylinder heads with 42mm XR Harley-Davidson inlet valves, and 38mm BMW exhaust valves. A factory oil cooler kit was ordered, but as this didn't arrive they manufactured their own out of Volkswagen parts. Instead of standard Conti mufflers megaphones were built using standard muffler shells.

In the 1976 AMA Superbike race at Daytona the California Hot Rod posted the fastest trap speed of 145.2mph (233.6kmh) and finished third behind the Monoshock BMW of Steve McLaughlin and twin-shock BMW of Pridmore. Throughout the season Neilson improved solidly, finishing second at the final meeting at Riverside. By this stage Morris magnesium wheels and attention paid to saving weight saw the machine trimmed down to 398lb (180kg), 25lb (11.3kg) lighter than before. It would lose another 28lb (12.7kg) before the 1977 season, fronting at Daytona weighing only 370lb (168kg). A close ratio gearbox was also installed to aid acceleration, and after the special factory gearbox failed Marvin Webster – known for building gear sets for Indianapolis race cars – was asked to build a more durable transmission for 1977.

By 1977 the California Hot Rod was approaching the peak of its development, and with heavy magazine commitments Neilson and Schilling decided to concentrate on winning the biggest race of the year, the Daytona Superbike event, rather than contest the entire championship. A general freshen up saw Neilson's 1974 750 SS engine cases and frame replace the now weary pre-production SS items, and the cylinder heads went back to Branch. He sank the valve seats, to accommodate 44mm Harley XR inlet valves and 38mm BMW exhausts without touching on overlap. Further port refinement yielded seven per cent flow increase. Along with new 10:1 Venolia pistons there was a new exhaust system with larger diameter headers and special megaphones developed through dragstrip testing. On the Axtell dyno before Daytona the California Hot Rod produced 90.4bhp at 8,300rpm. Yet while this was impressive for a Ducati twin the Yoshimura Kawasaki Z1s had a reputed 120bhp, and things looked ominous for California Hot Rod.

Fortunately for Neilson and Schilling events conspired in their favour. 'Just days before Daytona, Pops Yoshimura's Hollywood facility had a disastrous fire. It badly burned Pops Yoshimura, destroyed the engine dyno and the 120-horse engine, and stopped any further bike development before Daytona,' says Schilling. 'Heroically, Fujio Yoshimura assembled another engine, bolted the Kawasaki together, and got to Daytona.'

Neilson on the California Hot Rod during 1976. At this stage it was still based on the pre-production 1973 750 Super Sport. *(Fred Fitzgerald)*

Schilling with the California Hot Rod at Daytona in 1977, lighter and more powerful than before. *(Author's Collection)*

PIVOTAL SUCCESS: IMOLA AND DAYTONA **73**

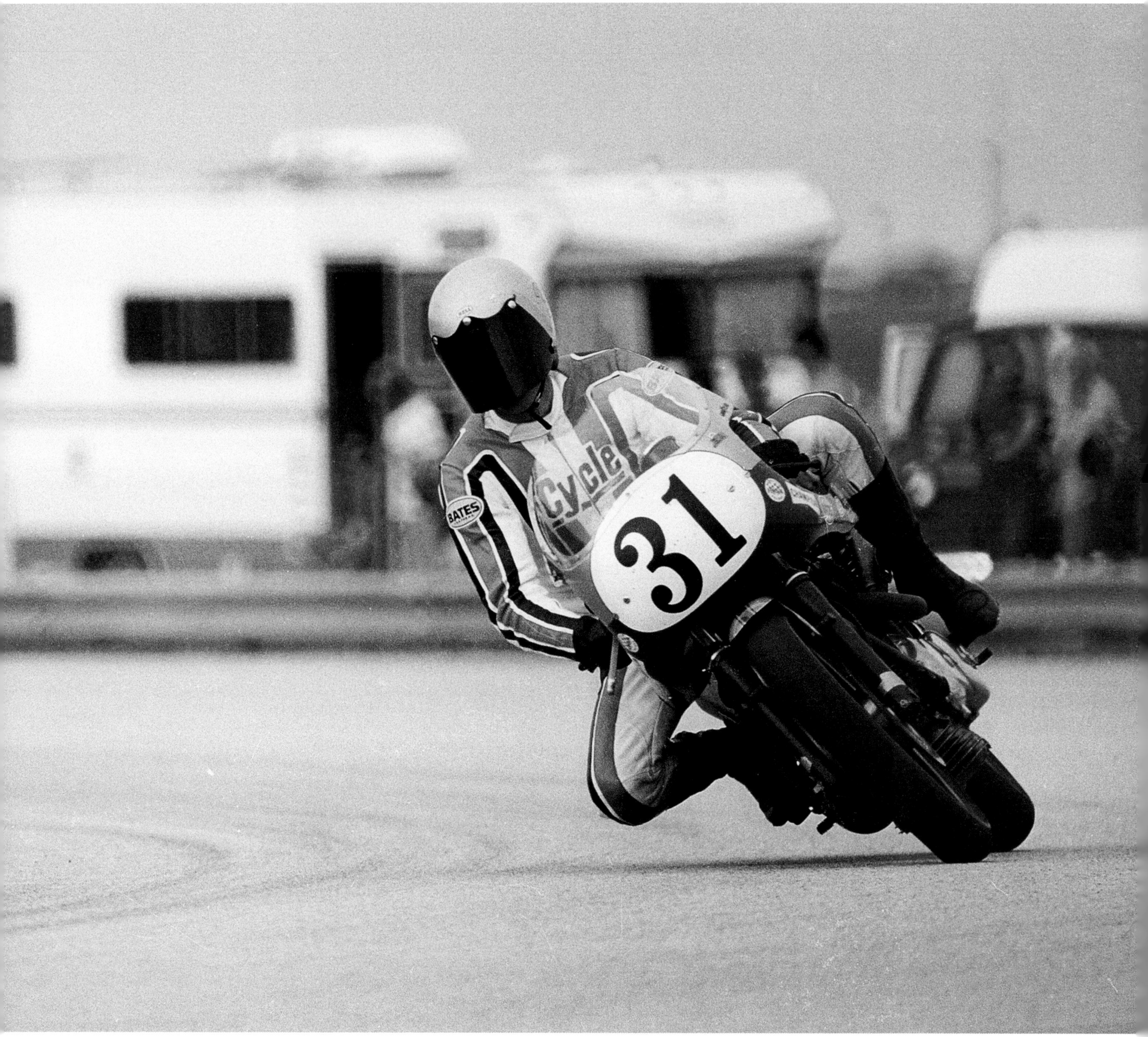
Cycle
31
BATES

Left: After Daytona Neilson only raced in selected Superbike events during 1977, including here at Laguna Seca in September. *(Cycle World)*

Opposite: In the 1977 Daytona Superbike race Neilson cleared away to provide Ducati their greatest victory ever in America. *(Author's Collection)*

For 1977 the AMA also adopted a stricter view towards chassis modifications. After the monoshock BMWs had obliterated all before them in 1976 such modifications were no longer allowed. This was also advantageous to the Ducati, as the stock Japanese frames were severely taxed by Superbike horsepower.

Despite these disadvantages the Yoshimura Kawasaki still posted the fasted speed through the traps in practice at 153mph (246kmh). The California Hot Rod was second at 149.5mph (240.5kmh), this year well ahead of the BMWs. Neilson knew that in the 50-mile (80.5km) Superbike race he had to clear away from the Kawasakis to make the most of the Ducati's cornering advantage. The danger was that the Kawasakis could draft past the Ducati at the finish line if they were too close coming out of the final chicane on to the bowl on the final lap. However, by the second lap Neilson had found the break he needed and he won from Dave Emde and Wes Cooley by 29 seconds. His average speed was 100.982mph (162.480kmh), with the fastest lap at 102.5mph (164.9kmh). This average speed would have been fast enough to win the Daytona Superbike race the following year as well. 'Not bad for a couple of amateurs,' quipped Schilling after the race. It was Ducati's greatest triumph since Imola in 1972, and the most important ever in America. Despite an absence of factory support the company also received unprecedented publicity. After Daytona the factory supplied Neilson and Schilling with a pair of unfinished 60° cylinder heads along with 905cc cylinders and pistons, but it was too late. They had achieved what they set out to do, and knew that factory parts alone were no guarantee of success.

The California Hot Rod was as much a victory for the Southern California hot-rod culture as it was for Ducati. The machine was subsequently sold to Dale Newton, who put the chassis aside and installed the engine in another set of running gear for his rider Paul Ritter. Ritter won the AMA Superbike race at Sears Point in 1977, beating Neilson, on Dale Newton's 860cc racer. This machine started life as a 1976 900 SS and was considerably more standard than the California Hot Rod. Armed with two race-winning Ducatis for 1978, Ritter found 'my old bike had a lot of low and mid-range torque but ran out of breath at 8,000rpm. Cook's bike didn't accelerate as hard but was really strong in the top-end, through until 9,400rpm.' After the California Hot-Rod engine's crankshaft failed at Daytona, Ritter chose to race the 1977 bike (now 883cc) at Sears Point, and won again. Dale Newton also set about building the 905cc engine with the 60° heads, Ritter managing second in the final 1978 AMA Superbike race at Laguna Seca. Ritter finished third in the championship.

COOK NEILSON AND PHIL SCHILLING

Few journalists manage to attain legendary status, but when Cook Neilson thundered across the line at Daytona in 1977 the names of Neilson and Schilling were synonymous with Ducati in America. Neilson was born in August 1943, and when he joined *Cycle* magazine in the late 1960s he came as a Princeton graduate, a noted motorcycle drag-racer (on nitro-burning Harley-Davidsons), and a member of the exclusive Bonneville 200-mph Club. As editor-in-chief, in 1972 he managed to move *Cycle* magazine's editorial offices from New York City to Westlake Village in Southern California. Here the magazine flourished, soon becoming the world's most influential motorcycle periodical. After exploring the limits of the canyons in the nearby Malibu Mountains, Neilson was also drawn into road racing, and, in the words of his friend Phil Schilling, 'Cook had a strong personal drive to go fast, and then faster. He was a natural competitor. Whatever the task or challenge, he wanted to stand out. Riding motorcycles well wouldn't suffice; he had to excel.' This culminated in the Daytona Superbike win and *Cycle* magazine's 'Beyond Racer Road' series that created the nucleus of the Ducati legend in America. Neilson retired from journalism in 1979, returning to the East Coast to pursue a photographic career. In 1997, on the 20th anniversary of the Daytona victory, he came out of retirement to ride the California Hot Rod in three demonstration laps at Daytona, still running at an impressive 145mph (233kmh).

Although Neilson earned the accolades, the victory wouldn't have happened without the talents of Phil Schilling. Schilling was born in Fort Wayne, Indiana, on 2 October 1940, and came to *Cycle* magazine as a refugee from graduate school, where he was working on a doctorate in American history. Involved in race tuning Ducati singles from 1964, Schilling also gained experience working with two-stroke Yamaha 250 and 350 racers, and a Kawasaki H1-R until 1970.

The impetus for the Daytona victory lay back at Imola in 1972. Schilling attended that race and immediately afterwards was promised one of the first production 750 Super Sports. 'That machine arrived nearly two years later, in December 1973, and was one of the three pre-production 750 SSs with 750 Sport engine and frame numbers that came to the US,' says Schilling. This 750 SS was transformed into 'Overdog' and the California Hot Rod. In an era when even factory endurance racers were struggling to be competitive against the Japanese fours it was amazing that Schilling could create a competitive racer without access to factory components. Schilling says: 'I think my expertise lay in polishing and praying, and hoping I got things put back correctly and more precisely than before.' In 1977 the California Hot Rod was unquestionably the fastest Ducati in the world, making Schilling one of the all-time great Ducati mechanics. He is remarkably modest about his achievement, saying 'I really think Cook could have succeeded without me. Standard parts lovingly put together was my motto and that Ducati engine went together like a fine watch.' Neilson disagrees on the matter of Schilling's importance. 'There's no way any of this would have worked without Phil. He was at the heart of any and all decisions made concerning the bike. While I did some of the pre-race preparation, I hardly touched the bike once we got to the track. It was all his. Besides, I had little knowledge of anything that went on below the cylinder base gaskets. All those gears and shafts that have to be shimmed so carefully? Schilling did all that. It's true that the engine went together like a fine watch. Phil was the watchmaker. I've never known a better one—and I've never had a better friend.' In 1979 he succeeded Neilson as *Cycle* magazine editor-in-chief, retiring in 1988.

Cook Neilson acknowledging his victory at Daytona. *(Author's Collection)*

Phil Schilling astride the California Hot Rod on the start line, next to the dominant BMWs, during 1976. *(Fred Fitzgerald)*

PIVOTAL SUCCESS: IMOLA AND DAYTONA **77**

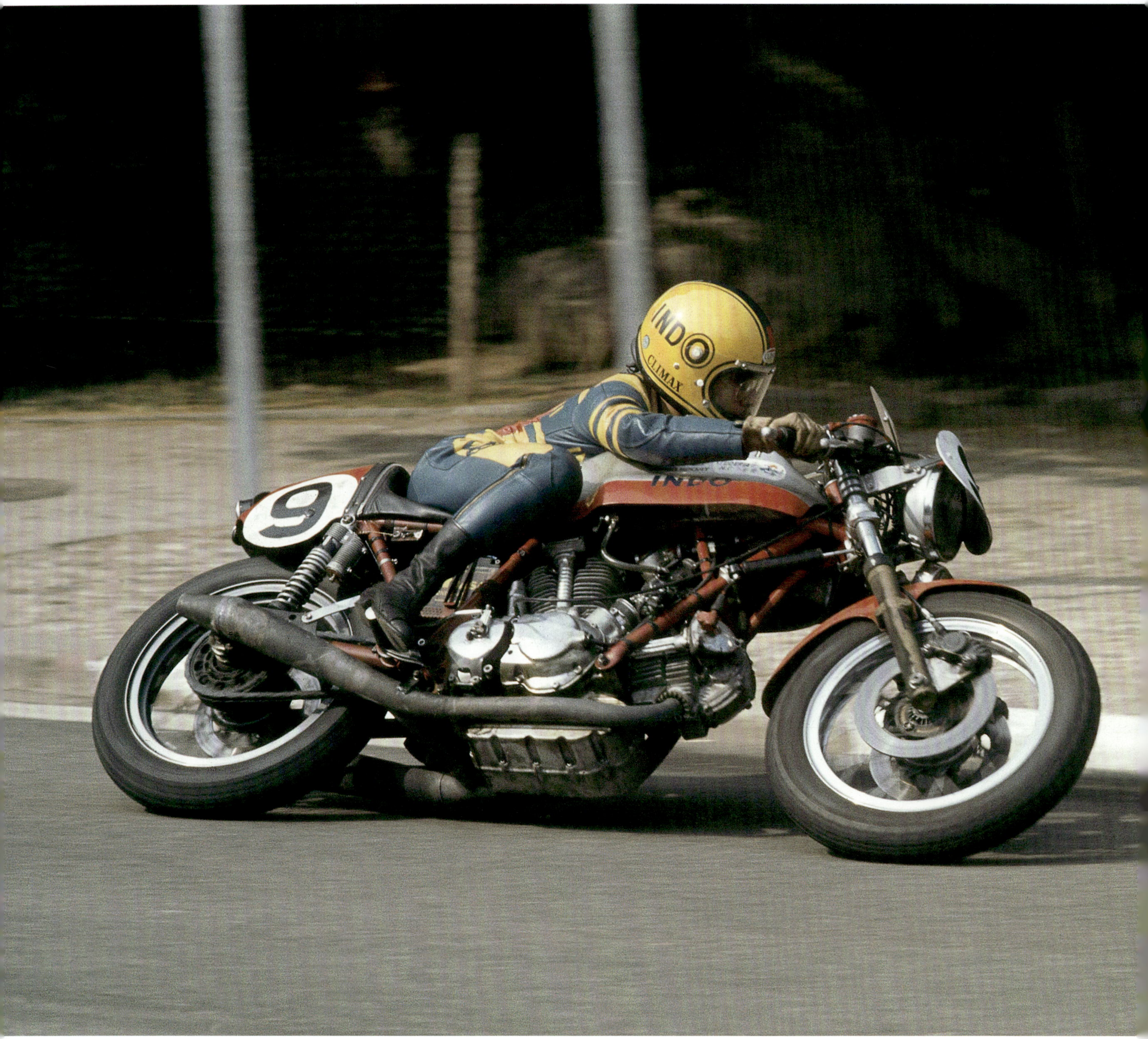
INDO
CLIMAX
9

5 THE NCR ERA: ENDURANCE AND FORMULA ONE

There was a new 905cc endurance racer for 1975, now with narrower crankcases and low exhaust pipes. Canellas (here) and Grau won at Barcelona, setting a new race record.
(Mick Woollett)

By 1973 endurance racing was really the only avenue left in which four-strokes were competitive. Even though the 1973 Imola racer was superb, and showed much promise, Taglioni knew it couldn't compete with the new liquid-cooled two-strokes. So, with the Barcelona 24 Hour race looming, soon after Imola Taglioni persuaded DeEccher to sanction official factory involvement. He argued that it would help in the development of a new larger capacity road bike as well as increase the company profile in Spain.

Rather than use modified 1973 Imola machines as originally intended, Taglioni decided on a larger engine to combat the Hondas and Kawasakis. Thus he created a racer around the production 750 chassis, with an 864cc engine achieved through combining the 1973 Imola racer's 86mm cylinders with the standard 74.4mm stroke. The crankcases were again the early sand-cast type with an additional sump bolt, and from the 1973 Imola bike came a dry clutch, 60° desmodromic cylinder heads, 40mm Dell'Orto carburettors, and high-rise exhaust system. There was a standard ignition distributor but with the condensers mounted on the front frame downtube. To aid reliability the compression ratio was reduced to 9:1 through concave 450 Scrambler pistons, and the power was 84–85bhp at 8,200rpm. Although the frame was ostensibly that of the 1973 750 Sport, the Scarab front and Lockheed rear brakes and Marzocchi forks were from the 1973

Benjamin Grau, with Salvador Canellas, gave the prototype 860 a debut victory at Montjuich in 1973. The dry clutch and 60° heads came from the 1973 Imola 750. *(Mick Woollett)*

Although not the most powerful, in the hands of specialists Canellas and Grau the 860 provided the best combination of power and handling. *(Mick Woollett)*

Imola bike. For this event there was a large fibreglass fuel tank, cooling scoop for the rear brake caliper, and only a small flyscreen fairing. Taglioni obviously wasn't concerned about ground clearance with the Dunlop TT100 tyres as the kick-start shaft was retained. As it transpired the 180kg (397lb) 860 prototype was eminently suited to the tight and twisting 3.62km (2.25-mile) Montjuich Park circuit. It may not have been the most powerful but the excellent handling and power characteristics of the 860 made it a formidable endurance racer, especially in the hands of local experts Salvador Canellas and 1972 race winner Benjamin Grau. For Ducati it was the 860's first win, and another victory on debut.

On 7 July 1973, with Taglioni in attendance, the Spanish pair took the lead in the Barcelona 24 Hour race on the third lap, relinquishing it only once to repair a punctured rear tyre. Eventually they won in record time, covering 1,674.58 miles (2,694.4km) at 71mph (114.2kmh), and leading home the second place Bultaco by 16 laps. Continuing Ducati's excellent record at Montjuich Park, it was also a magnificent debut for the 860. In September the same machine was entered for the Bol d'Or at Le Mans, though this time Canellas and Grau retired before half distance. During 1974 there was no longer any official factory racing involvement but Canellas and Grau were again supplied an 860 Desmo for the Barcelona 24 Hour. This was virtually the same as the previous year's machine, but with 90bhp and Lockheed front brakes. Again they were the strongest combination, leading by nine laps before retiring after 16 hours with a locked gearbox.

Even though the management discouraged racing, Taglioni and his department decided to mount a serious challenge to win the 1975 FIM Coupe d'Endurance. Running on a shoestring budget, and with machines entered through NCR, they very nearly succeeded. The series began at Montjuich on 5 July and Taglioni prepared an even more highly developed machine. With special sand-cast crankcases to allow tucked in exhaust pipes, the displacement was increased to 905cc through 88mm pistons. There were the usual 60° cylinder heads and dry clutch and the power was 96bhp at 9,000rpm, with 91.7bhp at 8,000rpm. Daspa created a special lightweight frame with additional bracing, and brakes were Lockheed front and rear. Canellas and Grau won yet again, covering 1,721.794 miles (2,770.965km) at an average speed of 71.74mph (115.45kmh). The machine ran like clockwork and they dominated the race, winning by 13 laps over the Godier–Genoud Kawasaki of Jacques Luc and Alain Vial. For the next round, the 1,000km at Mugello, Canellas wasn't available due to car rally driving commitments, so Virginio Ferrari partnered Grau. They won, but from then on results went awry. There were no points in Belgium, and at the Bol d'Or at Le Mans Grau crashed out on the first lap, restarting, but being eventually sidelined by gearbox seizure. The Bol d'Or machines featured Campagnolo cast magnesium wheels, a swingarm with rear eccentric chain adjustment, and a full fairing incorporating two large headlamps. The front brakes were Scarab or Lockheed, with a 280mm rear Brembo disc, and suspension was Marzocchi, with gas-filled rear shock absorbers. Grau went into the final round at Thruxton with a one-point lead, but a crash ended his chances and he finished third in the championship.

Canellas with the 1974 860cc endurance racer. Canellas and Grau were again the fastest combination but retired in the Barcelona 24-hour race. *(Museo Ducati)*

For the Thruxton 400-mile (643.6km) race two NCR racers were also supplied to British teams. Journalist Ray Knight rode one while Sports Motorcycles purchased another for Roger Nicholls and Steve Manship. 'It was definitely only 863.9cc and arrived from the factory with very low dished pistons,' says Steve Wynne. 'I think it had 60° heads and we changed the pistons to HC Omega.' These machines both featured narrow crankcases and a dry clutch. They also had a 24-litre (5.28-gallon) fibreglass tank with a clear strip, Daspa frames, Marzocchi ZTi forks, remote reservoir shock absorbers, Scarab front brakes and a Brembo rear disc. The Sports Motorcycles entry had Campagnolo magnesium wheels, and after leading the race early on a broken throttle cable put them out of contention.

By 1976 Franco Zauibouri had replaced DeEccher as general manager and brought a more positive attitude towards racing. Taglioni was barely on speaking terms with DeEccher but Zauibouri knew Taglioni's value to the company. Thus he sanctioned unofficial development of endurance racers in a bid to win the Coupe d'Endurance. Although entered by NCR, these were still factory racers, the budget increase immediately apparent in the improved presentation of the machines. Although favoured to win the Coupe d'Endurance this wasn't to be as the bikes were too fragile, and no one could have predicted the Honda onslaught that year.

As a warm up to the season, the first event for 1976 was the non-championship Bol d'Or d'Italia at Misano on 19 March. Here Virginio Ferrari and Carlo Perugini won on an NCR-entered 905cc machine similar to the 1975 endurance racers. This had a 24-litre fuel tank, a 1973-style fairing, and Brembo brakes. However, for the Coupe d'Endurance Ducati produced the classic 900 NCR, with its wonderfully sculptured fuel tank and seat unit. Only two machines were manufactured for this season, but they were spectacular in their attention to detail. The engines were still based on the round-case 750 design, with crankcases incorporating an oil level sight glass and machined engine covers. They had lightened straight-cut primary drive gears and special lightened crankshafts. The exhaust pipes were generally high-rise 'Imola' style. In the interest of improving reliability the displacement was reduced to 860cc, with 96bhp at 8,800rpm. There was also a shorter-stroke (88 x 70mm) 851cc engine that produced 93bhp at 8,600rpm. The compression ratio was a very moderate 9:1.

Although Taglioni's good friend Walter Villa, the younger brother of former works rider Francesco, tested a Campagnolo hydroconical front brake, this lacked power and forced the front forks apart. Thus the NCR featured 18-inch Campagnolo wheels with three 280mm Brembo discs. There was a duplex final drive and the weight was 156 kg (344lb). The season started well at Mugello, with Pentti Korhonen and Christian Estrosi finishing second. Then at Montjuich Ferrari and Grau retired, with the Spanish entry of Jose Mallol and Alejandro Tejedo on a 950cc machine ending third. With no other results, the 1976 endurance season ended in disappointment, and after the Bol d'Or Ducati officially withdrew from endurance racing.

Unofficially it was a different matter, and Taglioni still managed to provide support to NCR. However, with Grau heading for Honda, Ducati's prospects looked bleak for 1977. At the first round at Misano

The 1976 endurance racers were the first to feature the sculptured NCR tank and seat unit, but they were too fragile. (Carlo Perelli)

The only endurance racing success during 1978 was Grau and Canellas's win in the Silhouette class at the 24 Hour race at Le Mans in April. Their 900 SS was a modified production bike. (Museo Ducati)

on 5 June, Ermanno Giuliano and Giovanni Mariannini had an 808cc (88 x 66.5mm) racer that produced 92bhp at 8,700rpm. This continued to use the round-case bevel-drive layout, with points ignition, and there were narrower crankcases to allow lower (and shorter) exhausts. Piero Cavazzi developed a quick release system for the rear wheel and the weight was down to 148 kg (326lb). Giuliano and Mariannini came fourth, and after Misano Recchia revised the styling of the tailpiece, and there were now magnesium Marzocchi ZTi forks. However, while the line-up of five machines was impressive they were no match for the Honda RCB.

Although the new 900 NCR Formula 1 machines were the most successful NCR racers in 1978, four endurance racers were also produced. There was revised styling, combining a more integrated seat unit with the 24-litre fuel tank, and in many respects they were experimental racers. While the crankcases were similar to the F1 machines, on some examples there was now an electronic ignition running off the right end of the crankshaft. Several chassis configurations were tried during the year, including Daspa frames with eccentric adjustment at the swingarm. The endurance NCR racers also used radially drilled Brembo front discs, and some had duplex chain final drive and Campagnolo hydraulic conical rear brakes. The wheels were 2.50 and 3.00 x 18-inch magnesium Campagnolo.

The 1978 NCR endurance racers were impressive but unreliable. At the Misano Eight Hour race Marco Lucchinelli was leading until sidelined by ignition failure. Sauro Pazzaglia and Giovanni Mariannini came third. Benjamin Grau and Victor Palomo were running with the leading Honda at Montjuich but were slowed by a loose carburettor, eventually finishing sixth, while Estrosi and Boinet were up to second at one stage in the Bol d'Or before retiring. The most significant endurance racing result was Canellas and Grau's win in the Silhouette class at the 24 Hour race at Le Mans on 22–23 April, on an NCR-prepared 900 SS. They averaged 125.265kmh (201.551mph). This machine was ostensibly a production 900 Super Sport

Mario Recchia with the 1977 900 NCR. *(Museo Ducati)*

CASTROL
CASTROL
brembo
brembo
brembo
6
4
1
Agip
Agip
Agip
MICHELIN
MICHELIN

Left top: A single front disc with dual calipers was tested at Misano on the 1979 900 NCR. *(Museo Ducati)*

Opposite: A line-up of exquisite NCR endurance racers at Misano in May 1979. *(Museo Ducati)*

Left bottom: The 1979 machines also had a restyled fairing and seat, a square-section swingarm, and a re-routed left exhaust. *(Museo Ducati)*

For more than a decade Grau, often teamed with Canellas, was Ducati's most successful endurance racer. Grau and Canellas excelled at Montjuich, and rode the 900 NCR to third in 1979. The endurance racers this year ran the ignition off the crankshaft on the right. *(Museo Ducati)*

with a race-prepared engine and wider Campagnolo wheels to accept racing tyres. Amazingly it still ran with air cleaners!

The success of the Formula 1 900 NCR prompted renewed interest in endurance racing by the factory and for 1979 five new endurance machines were prepared. These still used the round-case bevel-drive layout, with spin-on oil filter, but there were new frames with square-section aluminium swingarms. Experimentation with brakes and suspension included a single front disc with twin brake calipers but this wasn't successful. There was also a new fairing and tailpiece. Despite the limited budget the NCRs were surprisingly competitive: Victor Palomo and Mario Lega came second at Assen and third at Nürburgring, while Canellas and Grau managed third at Montjuich after suffering handling problems.

There was no official factory involvement in the Coupe d'Endurance during 1980, but Jose Mallol and Alejandro Tejedo won the Barcelona 24 Hour race at Montjuich. On a modified 900 SS entered in the Silhouette Class by local importer Ricardo Fargas, they gave Ducati their first victory in the event since 1975. Only racing because it was also the final round of the Spanish Endurance Championship, they covered 757 laps at 74.12mph (119.3kmh). In the 1981 Barcelona race Mallol and Tejedo were slowed by wheel breakages, but Benjamin Grau and Enrique de Juan, on a 950 Ducati, covered 771 laps to take second place. This was on a modified square-case 900 SS, with a two-into-one exhaust, but it lacked many of the earlier special features of the NCR bikes. Then in 1982, Grau with Carlos Cardus came fourth at Montjuich. It was the 900 Ducati's final fling in endurance racing, but considering the design was 12 years old it was an impressive achievement.

Five spectacular 1977 900 NCR endurance racers, a line-up to make any Ducati enthusiast's mouth water. *(Museo Ducati)*

SCUDERIA NCR

During 1967, factory mechanics Giorgio Nepoti, Rino Caracchi, and Rinaldo Rizzi set up a specialist race shop (NCR). After Rizzi left NCR became Nepoti Caracchi Racing, and they assisted in the preparation of the 1972 Imola machines. Located in via Signorini 16, close to the factory at Borgo Panigale, NCR's first official race entry was a 750 Super Sport in the 1973 Imola 200, on which Claudio Loigo finished 15th. Eventually NCR became the unofficial factory racing team when, after the success at Montjuich in 1973, Fabio Taglioni was determined to persevere with a racing programme, even without the support of management. Teaming up with old friends seemed the obvious solution. Therefore the moderately successful endurance racers of 1975 were entered under the NCR banner, although they were still prepared by Franco Farnè, Mario Recchia, and Piero Cavazzi, alongside Nepoti and Caracchi.

With the increased endurance effort for 1976 the NCR machines became more specialised, and pure works of art. Caracchi, the master of the lathe and milling machine, created beautiful components such as the rear brake caliper support. Nepoti was responsible for the other strength of the NCR, its crankshaft. In the words of the great Italian-American Ducati tuner Reno Leoni 'the secret to the NCR was the crank. They had great crankshafts.' With factory support they were also able to create really spectacular endurance racing machines, sharing virtually nothing with any production Ducati.

Although most associated with the bevel-drive racers, NCR continue as leading tuners of racing Ducatis to the present day. They not only fielded Pantahs throughout the 1980s, but Nepoti and Caracchi also assisted Eraldo Ferracci and Doug Polen in 1991. Nepoti retired in 1995, but Rino Caracchi continues to operate from a workshop opposite the old site, and his son Stefano is involved in the current NCR World Superbike team.

TT FORMULA 1

Even though Taglioni still wanted to compete in the Coupe d'Endurance, he knew that in this highly competitive category the Ducatis would never beat the might of Honda. So he greeted the advent of the Tourist Trophy Formula 1 race at the Isle of Man with relish. Created in 1976 to save the Isle of Man races following the boycott by leading Grand Prix riders in 1975, this was for production-based machinery. A production run of 1,000 was required, and while the engine stroke had to be retained there were few restrictions regarding engine and chassis modifications. The exhaust had to pass 115 dB(A) at 11m (36.1ft), but this was the same as endurance regulations. Taglioni reasoned he could almost run endurance specification machines in TT F1, and the 900 would surely be competitive. Already in the 1976 production race at the Isle of Man, Roger Nicholls and Steve Tonkin, on a modified Sports Motorcycles entered 860cc 750 SS, had given some indication of the Ducati's suitability to the Island. Nicholls set a best lap of 103.13mph (165.96kmh) before retiring.

This result was good enough for Steve Wynne to persuade the factory to sell him a used 900 NCR endurance racer for the 1977 TT F1 race. He was assured their top mechanic Giuliano Pedretti would prepare the bike, but it was so slow in coming he eventually sent some friends to Bologna to collect it. When the 900 NCR arrived Steve was dismayed to find 'it was knackered, and looked as though it had done ten 24-hour races.' A call to Bologna saw Pedretti fly over with replacement parts and together with Wynne they rebuilt the engine so it performed faultlessly. This engine had narrower sand-cast crankcases and dry clutch, but 'to my recollection it didn't have 60° cylinder heads,' says Steve. The power was around 75–80bhp, and Nicholls almost beat the Honda of Phil Read. The race was shortened by a lap due to rain, and Honda, having got wind of this, cancelled their final fuel stop thus allowing Read to win by 39 seconds. However, Nicholls was the moral victor, and with the signing of Mike Hailwood for the 1978 F1 TT Ducati decided to produce a small number of 900 NCR Formula One machines.

Unlike the endurance racers, the Formula 1 900 NCR was a catalogued model, and according to Rino Caracchi 18 complete machines were built, along with 20 spare engines. They carried 900 SS engine numbers (in the 088 series) but featured specially-cast crankcases

STEVE WYNNE AND SPORTS MOTORCYCLES

One of the most important Ducati tuners, Steve Wynne set up Sports Motorcycles in 1965 as a repair shop but was soon one of the leading BSA, Triumph, and Norton retail outlets in Britain. Wynne was born on 4 October 1945 and left school without any qualifications to work as a maintenance and tool room fitter. A passion for motorcycles eventually led to him working at a used motorcycle dealership, and soon he founded Sports Motorcycles in Manchester. Following the demise of the British motorcycle industry, rather than turn to a Japanese franchise Steve tested a Ducati 750 GT. That marked the beginning of his love affair with the Bolognese marque.

Wynne took to the track, first with a 750 Sport, and later with a 750 SS, but realising that his talents lay in race preparation Wynne began to support riders such as Roger Nicholls and Steve Manship. By 1975 Sports Motorcycles were the leading Ducati race team in England, and in late 1977 John Sear joined the company as sales manager to allow Steve to concentrate on race preparation. Sear was a friend of Mike Hailwood but left the company in 1980 to seek more profitable employment. After the 1978 Isle of Man victory Pat Slinn joined the company, coming over from British distributors Coburn and Hughes, but he left when the company was downsized from 30 employees to two in 1982. Poor economic circumstances forced Steve to give his house back to the bank and live over the garage, but Sports Motorcycles survived and continued to prepare racing Ducatis, including the 1981 to 1983 TT-winning machines of Tony Rutter. Steve Wynne retired from race preparation following the death of his rider Robert Holden at the Isle of Man in 1996 on a 916 SP.

Although based on the round-case 750, the 1978 F1 900 NCR engine had many special components, and was very much a product of the racing department. *(Roy Kidney)*

incorporating a spin-on oil filter, and retained the earlier 750 bevel-drive layout with points ignition. The displacement was the same as the production 900 SS at 864cc (86 x 74.4mm), also with an 80° included valve angle. There were special 44 and 38mm nimonic valves, lighter 10:1 Borgo pistons, 12mm lift desmodromic camshafts, and a lightened crankshaft – 7.4kg (16.3lb) as opposed to 8kg (17.6lb) without the alternator. The con-rods were the same 150mm (5.9in) length as the round-case 750 rather than the shorter square-case rod, but with a 19mm gudgeon. The inlet ports were increased to 38mm, with the exhaust ports up to 34mm. The F1 900 NCR also featured a close ratio six-dog gearbox and straight cut primary gears (31/75) with a dry clutch, and with Dell'Orto 40mm carburettors produced 92bhp at 8,500rpm. To keep the 4kg (8.8lb) of oil at 110°C there was also an oil cooling system, with a Citroën oil radiator and crankshaft feed through the aluminium primary drive cover. F1 900 NCR production ran from 1977 until 1979.

The Daspa frame weighed 12kg (26.5lb) and the suspension, wheels and brakes were less exotic than on the endurance machines. Cavazzi's quick release wheel system and milled brake caliper mount were absent, as were the magnesium forks and shock absorbers. The Marzocchi forks were also considerably narrower at 180mm (7.1in) rather than the 195mm (7.7in) of the street bike. There were still some nice touches though, such as the vernier adjusters for the milled foot levers. The overall weight was only 160kg (353lb). A special Formula 1 machine was built for Mike Hailwood with a left-side gearshift conversion via a crossover shaft through the swingarm pivot. This was because Hailwood suffered severe damage to his right foot in a Formula 2 racing accident at the Nürburgring in 1974. Steve Wynne completely reworked the heads and valves (installing a 40mm exhaust), incorporated a Lucas Rita electronic ignition, and Venolia 11:1 Teflon-lined pistons sourced from Neilson and Schilling in California. Unable to get them to seal properly he then used Omega. Other changes included Girling shock absorbers, and carbon fibre bodywork. He also changed the clutch and with Hailwood's help had Hewland Gears redesign and manufacture a complete gear set, still with six engagement dogs but of an improved design.

Steve Wynne found, just as Cook Neilson and Phil Schilling had, that the gearbox was the Achilles heel of these engines, but eventually the factory took notice and incorporated some of these design improvements in the

Like the endurance machines, the F1 900 NCR had a Daspa frame with additional bracing. There were also narrower crankcases with a spin-on oil filter, and a dry clutch.
(Roy Kidney)

There was a new F1 machine for Hailwood in 1979, and he tested this at Misano before the TT. Despite the new frame and swingarm the machine handled poorly, and for the TT Steve Wynne substituted the 1978 Daspa frame.
(Museo Ducati)

90 DUCATI RACERS

Hailwood's 1978 TT winning machine (088238) went to Japan, and in the mid-1990s to the US. Here it has a right-side gearshift, although Hailwood used a left shift. *(Roy Kidney)*

THE 1978 MIKE HAILWOOD FORMULA 1 900 NCR

The two NCR 900s that Sports Motorcycles received in 1978 were Mike Hailwood's machine, with engine 088238, and Roger Nicholls's, number 088239. Hailwood did all the pre-TT and official practice through until the Friday evening with engine 088238, but for the final practice and race Wynne installed a new engine, 088243, that he had asked Ducati to ship in at the last minute. 'I paid for Farnè and Pedretti to came over with the engine and they were worried the original engine had too many miles on it. I think they may also have had some failures,' says Wynne. 'This new engine had none of my mods, except a Lucas Rita ignition.'

After the race it was found the bottom bevel gear had sheared as it crossed the finish line, so the original engine (088238) was installed for the Mallory Park, Donington, and Silverstone races. At the end of the 1978 season Steve Wynne sold the Hailwood bike (with engine 088238) to Mr Hiyashi in Japan for £5,000. Coburn and Hughes retained Nicholls's machine (088239) and sold it to Wolfgang Reiss in Hanover, Germany, with a certificate describing it as the Hailwood bike (complete with a left-side gearshift conversion).

The spare engine that won the race (088243) was later totally rebuilt by Steve Wynne, who says 'it had a different crank, gearbox, 90mm pistons, and the only parts left were the crankcases.' Wynne installed this engine in the 1979 chassis and raced it in the 1981 Daytona Battle of the Twins race. Here the crankcases split, 'most likely because I machined too much out to fit the big bore.' This engine remained in the US thereafter and was eventually placed in an NCR 900 chassis. Larry Auriana ended up with the complete collection, not only buying 088238 but also purchasing the Nicholls bike (088239) and the engine that won the Isle of Man TT (088243). Scaysbrook's NCR went to Australia, where it was raced for many years, including a ride by Wayne Gardner in the 1980 Coca Cola Eight Hour race.

MIKE HAILWOOD'S RETURN TO THE ISLE OF MAN

Wandering around the pits at Silverstone in August 1977 Mike Hailwood spotted the Sports Motorcycles NCR 900 that Nicholls had raced at the Isle of Man. He swung a leg over it and commented that this was the kind of old-fashioned bike he liked, and would enjoy at the Isle of Man. Within ten minutes, Hailwood had shaken hands with Vernon Cooper of the ACU and committed himself to ride in the 1978 TT. Hailwood had stopped racing motorcycles in 1972, but made a return on a Manx Norton in some Australian historic races early in 1977. Though he had originally wanted to ride anonymously he arranged with Wynne at Silverstone for him to supply a Ducati for the Formula 1 TT, and on 30 September the deal was signed. Hailwood would only receive £1,000 and the company would have unlimited use of Hailwood's name for advertising. To acclimatise himself to a Ducati he then rode a production 750 SS in the Australian Castrol Six Hour race with Jim Scaysbrook, finishing sixth. Another outing on the 750 SS in the Adelaide Three Hour race saw the pair seventh. Ducati agreed to provide special Formula 1 machines and, atypically for Ducati, two arrived in plenty of time and were with Sports Motorcycles in Manchester by the beginning of 1978.

At that time Hailwood was living in New Zealand and flew back to England to test the 900 NCR at Oulton Park in early May. On 22 May he travelled to the Isle of Man in preparation for the most anticipated comeback ever. Mike was 38 years old and hadn't raced at the Island for 11 years. He was fastest in practice with a lap of 111.04mph (178.66kmh) and would start as race favourite, and on Saturday 3 June 1978, just after 4:00 pm, Hailwood set off to cover the six laps of the 37.73-mile (60.71km) Isle of Man circuit. Starting 50 seconds after Phil Read on the works Honda, Hailwood had caught up with him by the third lap. Nicholls had already retired on the first lap when the oil level window split, and after the pit stop Hailwood overtook Read on the track. Read retired on lap five, and in front of the largest crowd on the Island in more than a decade Hailwood cruised home to win by two minutes at an average speed of 108.51mph (174.59kmh). His fastest lap was 110.62mph (177.99kmh). It was an astounding victory and vindication, not only of Hailwood's extraordinary ability, but also of the brilliant balance of power and handling of the 900 NCR. Just like Imola, the Isle of Man success would be pivotal in the racing history of Ducati. It was Ducati's first World Championship, and fittingly Mike Hailwood was their first World Champion.

As if to prove the Isle of Man race was no fluke, the following week Hailwood gave the Ducati an even more astonishing victory at the post-TT meeting at Mallory Park, on 11 June. Here, despite a clear horsepower deficiency and after a slow start, he overtook both Read and the P&M Kawasaki of John Cowie to score an easy win at 93.18mph (149.93kmh). A month after Mallory Hailwood rode the Ducati in the Formula 1 race at Donington, setting a fastest lap of 88.744mph (142.819kmh) before crashing. His final race on the F1 Ducati for 1978 was at Silverstone on 6 August, where he finished third. Although outpowered again, Hailwood still managed a 110mph (177kmh) lap. In October he again shared a 750 SS with Scaysbrook in the Castrol Six Hour race in Australia, but this time Scaysbrook crashed.

Hailwood returned to live in Britain in 1979, and signed to ride a Ducati in both the Formula 1 and Classic TTs. However, at the official practice session at Misano his bike was fitted with a reverse direction gearshift by mistake and he crashed towards the end of the two-day test session while inadvertently selecting the wrong gear. Escaping with two cracked ribs, this made front page news in Italy. Then, only days before the race, Ducati's directors decided not to send the bikes to the Isle of Man as they were worried about insurance liability. Steve Wynne then agreed to purchase the F1 machine but didn't expect the machine for the Classic. Later Farnè, Rino Caracchi, and development engineer Renzo Neri also flew out.

Unfortunately the new bike was disappointing and in practice Hailwood could only lap at 105.88mph (170.36kmh). Even though he felt he was going much faster than the previous year it was hard work. Although he still rode his heart out in the Formula 1 race he lost fifth gear, the battery carrier broke, and an exhaust pipe began to fall off. Hailwood stopped at Hilberry to reconnect the battery and finished a creditable fifth, at an average speed of 106.06mph (170.65kmh) with a fastest lap of 109.45mph (176.11kmh). So disillusioned was Hailwood with the Ducati that he decided not to race it at any of the post-TT meetings. He said later that he felt Ducati had let him down in 1979, and after the wonderful result in 1978 he certainly had a right to feel disheartened.

Hailwood on the start line at the Isle of Man, 3 June 1978. His win gave Ducati their first World Championship and marked a fairytale comeback. *(Mick Woollett)*

Proving any detractors wrong, Hailwood rode the F1 Ducati to victory at Mallory Park a week later. Here he leads Phil Read. *(Mick Woollett)*

THE NCR ERA: ENDURANCE AND FORMULA ONE

Sauro Pazzaglia raced this 950cc NCR Superbike in the 1981 Italian Superbike series. *(Museo Ducati)*

production bikes. Additional 900 NCR F1 machines were supplied to Nicholls, and Jim Scaysbrook from Australia (through Frasers, the New South Wales importer). Eddie Roberts lined up on the older NCR bike, now with 10:1 Omega pistons. By the time the team made it to the Island the traditional NCR colours of red and silver had been replaced by Castrol colours of red, white, and green on all except Scaysbrook's machine.

So pleased were they with the 1978 result that Ducati decided to support an official team for the 1979 Formula 1 and Classic TT. New machines were produced, but there were the inevitable delays and it was only two weeks before the TT that the official practice session was held at Misano. TT F1 regulations changed so the special sand-cast narrow crankcases with the oil filter were no longer allowed. Therefore the engine was now based on the standard die-cast square-case 900 SS, without a dry clutch, and remained at 864cc. The Classic TT racer used an endurance type engine with special crankcases and dry clutch, but with square-case 900 bevel gear distribution. It was rumoured to displace 947cc (with 90mm pistons and Gilnisil cylinders). There were new Dell'Orto 40mm carburettors featuring very short and wide bell mouths, and the claimed power was an optimistic 115bhp. Both the F1 and Classic machine featured a new Daspa frame, altered fairing shape, and a revised tail section. This frame not only raised the engine to give more ground clearance but the steering head angle was steeper than the earlier 29.5°. They also had a square-section aluminium swingarm to allow for a wider rear tyre, a high routed left exhaust pipe, and the Cavazzi quick release rear wheel set-up. There were also new adjustable Marzocchi forks, with magnesium fork legs on the endurance machines.

As Hailwood damaged one of the two F1 machines in the crash at Misano, one F1 (with a spare engine) and one Classic machine were sent to the Isle of Man for Hailwood, arriving only a few days before the race. Despite the factory involvement, the 1979 F1 machine was vastly inferior to that of the previous year. According to Wynne 'it was basically a standard 900 SS with an Imola cam. We installed the spare engine with a special cam halfway through practice week but it blew to bits after half a lap.' Not only was the bike down on power but it handled so poorly that Steve Wynne sent for Nicholls's 1978 machine, then on display in the Coburn and Hughes showroom. Although it was of dubious legality, at the instigation of Ducati Wynne installed the 1978 model frame with narrower round-section swingarm.

The Classic machine too was disappointing. Hailwood declared it 'unrideable' after one lap and elected to ride a Suzuki RG 500 in the Classic. George Fogarty (Carl's father) rode the 947 in the Classic, now with a heavily modified frame, but crashed badly at Signpost Corner. In addition to Hailwood's official Isle of Man machine Sports Motorcycles also prepared an F1 racer for Fogarty. With standard 750 round-case crankcases, Wynne incorporated many parts from the older NCR racer. The pistons were 90mm Omega giving a 10:1 compression ratio. The crankshaft and milled con-rods were from the 1974 750 SS, but with a 38mm (up from 36mm) crankpin and 3mm needle roller bearings. There were also the straight-cut primary gears and dry clutch with sintered bronze friction plates. One of Wynne's most effective modifications was to remove three gearbox dogs, and eventually the factory followed suit on their production bikes. The NCR Daspa frame was basically unchanged but the swingarm incorporated eccentric adjusters at the axle, and the footpegs were also mounted on eccentrics. On this machine Fogarty finished seventh in the F1 TT.

Although the Formula 1 Ducatis were outclassed by 1980, Vanes Francini was provided with a factory machine for the Italian Regions Trophy TT 1 Championship. This had fully floating disc brakes, FPS wheels, and a revised exhaust system, and Francini won three races to take the championship. Steve Wynne continued to develop the Sports Motorcycles Formula 1 machine and had Ron Williams reinforce the frame. With a special Dr Roe exhaust system, 12:1 90mm Omega pistons, 44 and 40mm valves, and 40mm Lectron flat slide carburettors, the engine produced 90bhp at the rear wheel. However, this wasn't enough to make the 159kg (350lb) machine competitive.

By 1981 the emerging Superbike class had overtaken Formula 1 and NCR prepared a 947cc 900 SS-based Superbike for Sauro Pazzaglia in the Italian series. A 900 TT1/Coupe d'Endurance machine was also displayed at the 1981 Bologna Show. This featured a square-case engine with electric start, but by now the bevel-twin just wasn't competitive and Taglioni turned to a Pantah-based TT1 racer during 1982.

Jimmy Adamo won three Battle of the Twins Championships in the US in the early 1980s on Reno Leoni's bevel-drive racer. Leoni and Adamo pose with their 1985 Cagiva Alazzurra. Adamo, winner of 32 twins-class victories, was tragically killed at Daytona in 1993. *(Australian Motorcycle News)*

BATTLE OF THE TWINS

By 1979 the bevel-drive Ducati was struggling against the increased professionalism of the Japanese in AMA Superbike racing. Freddie Spencer rode the Reno Leoni-prepared NCR at Daytona, and Richard Schlachter won at Loudon in June on George Vincensi's 900 square-case racer. That really marked the end of the era for twins in AMA Superbike and led to the establishment of a new race series titled the Battle of the Twins. After a trial race in October 1980, the 11-race series kicked off at Daytona in March 1981. Immediately the Reno Leoni-tuned Ducati of Jimmy Adamo dominated the GP class. His square-case 860 produced 96–98bhp at 9,000rpm, the 80° cylinder heads featured 44 and 39mm valves, and the carburettors were 41mm Malossi. Adamo won the race at 101.106mph (162.679kmh) and second was Schlachter on the George Vincensi round-case racer. Adamo won the series in 1981 and continued to dominate Battle of the Twins in 1982 and 1983, his 989cc (with 92mm pistons) machine now producing nearly 100bhp at 9,000rpm. Although their 145kg (320lb), 947cc bevel-drive twin produced 110bhp at 8,500rpm by 1984, Leoni and Adamo raced a Cagiva Pantah during 1985. Then for 1986 Leoni reverted to the bevel-drive Mille, boring the engine to 1,017cc. Producing more than 100bhp at the rear wheel, and running 16-inch wheels, Adamo even led the 1987 Daytona BOTT race before retiring. The success of Battle of the Twins soon saw it established in the UK and Europe. In 1982 Dave Railton set the pace on his 950 bevel-twin, but by 1983 Tony Rutter was showing the way on a 750 TT1.

brembo
MARZOCCHI
DUCATI
MICHELIN
Agip
DUCATI
MICHELIN
brembo

6 RACING PANTAHS

For the 1980 Junior Italian TT2 Championship four factory racers were prepared. Based on the 500 SL Pantah, they dominated the championship. *(Museo Ducati)*

As the racing flame of the bevel-drive twin waned it was Fabio Taglioni's next generation engine, the Pantah, which upheld Ducati's racing honour. When it first appeared during 1977 as a 500, the Pantah wasn't considered for racing development as there was no suitable racing class. The bevel-drive 900 was also continuing to provide success, but it was at the peak of its development. As the Japanese overcame the handling deficiencies of their larger machines the 900 Ducati lost its advantage and after 1980 there was little success for the venerable bevel-drive racers.

Taglioni's hands were also tied when Ducati became part of Finmeccanica in the VM Group during 1980. VM were more interested in manufacturing diesels and considered motorcycle production secondary. Taglioni too seemed to have little interest in developing the production range, and motorcycle manufacture slipped from 6,838 in 1981 to an all-time low of 1,765 in 1984. This wasn't a good time at Borgo Panigale. Even so, though times were grim at the factory Taglioni persevered with development of the racing Pantah. In many ways the Pantah was an updated amalgam of the earlier 500cc Grand Prix machine and the Armaroli version. It shared the same 74 x 58mm bore and stroke, but the Pantah was much more modern, and an exceptionally strong design. Some of the new design characteristics were foreign to Taglioni, particularly the forged one-piece crankshaft. Although he envisaged the concept, he entrusted all the

Massimo Broccoli gave the TT2 a debut win in 1981, going on to win the Junior Italian TT F2 Championship. *(Museo Ducati)*

actual design work to Gianluigi Mengoli and Renzo Neri. When it came to the cylinder head design they settled on two desmodromic valves set at the 60° included angle that worked so admirably during the 1970s. The toothed belt camshaft drive was lighter than the bevel gears, and with the swingarm pivoting on the rear of the crankcases the engine could be placed in a shorter chassis.

The initial production Pantah trellis frame wasn't noted for its compactness or rigidity, but for the 1980 Junior Italian TT2 Championship Franco Farnè and the racing department prepared four race-kitted Pantahs. An 80mm piston took the capacity to 583cc, and with racing camshafts, 36mm Dell'Orto carburettors, and a Verlicchi two-into-one exhaust they produced 70bhp at 9,000rpm. The suspension was magnesium Marzocchi, 35mm adjustable forks and remote reservoir shock absorbers, and Brembo brakes with twin 260mm front discs and 05 calipers. The wheels were 18-inch, either magnesium Speedline or aluminium FPS. With bodywork patterned on the 900 NCR these machines were incredibly successful, and in the hands of Vanes Francini, Pietro Menchini, and Guido Del Piano they won 12 Junior TT2 races. Del Piano took the championship, and this success prompted Fabio Taglioni to release the magnificent TT2 for 1981.

THE 600CC TT2

For 1981 the Italian Junior Championship was run to TT Formula 2 regulations. This allowed production-based 251–350cc two-strokes and 401–600cc four-strokes, with freedom regarding chassis. With this in mind, Taglioni produced what was possibly the definitive air-cooled twin-cylinder racer for the 1981 Italian series. Although utilising production Pantah castings, the factory TT2 engine was bored to 81mm to provide 598cc. There were Gilnisil cylinders and two-ring 10:1 AE Borgo pistons weighing 408g (14.3oz). The forged 124mm (4.9in) con-rod was highly polished, as was the lightened crankshaft, and there were straight-cut (36/70) primary gears, a 16 plate dry clutch, and close ratio five-speed gearbox. The clutch operation was hydraulic and there was a magnesium primary drive cover. The ignition was standard Bosch BTZ with 32° advance, and the TT2 retained the electric start and alternator. In the cylinder head the valves were increased to 41mm inlet and 35mm exhaust, and racing camshafts provided 12mm of intake lift and 10mm exhaust. Italian regulations allowed Dell'Orto PHM 40mm carburettors,

98 DUCATI RACERS

and the power was 76bhp at 10,750rpm. A bypass oil cooler was also fitted, cooling oil to the cylinder heads.

Even more spectacular than the engine was the triangulated 8kg (17.6lb) chrome-molybdenum Verlicchi frame. This fitted the engine so closely there was no room for timing belt covers, and it still used the engine as a stressed member, with stronger butt-fitted bosses rather than flat tabs as on the production frame. The fork rake was reduced from 30° to 24°. There was no lower engine support, the tubular steel swingarm pivoting on the rear crankcase. The cantilever single Paioli shock absorber may not have been state-of-the-art but it was extremely effective. The forks were 35mm fully adjustable Marzocchi with magnesium fork legs, and the front brakes fully floating 260mm Brembo with gold series 05 calipers. At the rear was a 260mm plasma-sprayed Zinzani alloy disc. With Campagnolo 2.15 and 3.00 x 18-inch magnesium wheels the TT2 was diminutive. As the claimed weight was only 130kg (287lb) and it rode on a 1,370mm (4ft 5.9in) wheelbase, the TT2 was really more reminiscent of the single cylinder racers than the larger V-twins.

1981

The TT2's first race was at Misano on 29 March 1981, Massimo Broccoli winning the event. This victory placed the TT2 in the illustrious company of the Marianna, 125 Desmo, and Imola 750, which had all won on their debut appearances. To further emphasise the TT2's brilliance Broccoli went on to win the 1981 Junior Italian TT F2 Championship. He was also supplied a 500cc version for the final round of the Italian 500 series at Mugello in October 1981, finishing an impressive seventh in a field of 500 GP Suzukis and Yamahas.

After all their bevel-drive machines retired in the 1980 TT, Sports Motorcycles also decided to switch their allegiance to the Pantah for 1981. At the 1980 Cologne Show Ducati promised them two works engines for the Isle of Man Formula 2 TT in June. Sports would need to provide the chassis and there would be no factory mechanic. An engine duly arrived but, true to form, this was well worn, and only 500cc. Lacking sponsorship, Steve Wynne was found a 500SL Pantah insurance write-off and in January asked Tony Rutter to ride. Rutter agreed to ride without payment, and a Ducati Owners'

One of the Pantah Ice Trophy racers in action during 1982. *(Museo Ducati)*

PANTAH ICE TROPHY RACER

One of the more unusual racing Ducatis was a 500cc Pantah created for the European Ice Trophy during 1981. Based on the street 500 SL, ten of these machines were built, producing 52bhp at 9,000rpm. The Pantah Ice Trophy was first displayed at the 1981 Bologna Show as a joint Ducati/Alfa Romeo project – Ducati were to supply Pantah racers, and Alfa Romeo Alfa Sud cars. Although fitted with special spiked 18-inch tyres (190 on the front and 235 on the rear) on FPS wheels, the Pantah Ice Trophy Racer specification was remarkably similar to that of the road bike, but there was only a single 260mm front disc brake. The Austrian rider Hans Maier raced one during 1982.

TONY RUTTER

Not many road racers can claim to have won their first World Championship at the age of 39 but that is exactly what Tony Rutter did when he won the 1981 World TT Formula 2 Championship. It was the first of four consecutive World Championships until a tragic accident prematurely ended his career. While he may have made his international name on Ducatis, Tony Rutter was already almost a 20-year veteran of the British short-circuit championships by the time he stepped aboard the Sports Motorcycles Pantah in 1981. His first race was at Brands Hatch in 1962 on a 350cc BSA Gold Star, soon graduating to a Manx Norton. It was after his first visit to the Isle of Man in 1965, where he finished 41st in the 350 Junior, that he developed the taste for road racing.

One of the first privateers to embrace the switch to two-strokes, Rutter raced Yamahas from 1968, winning his first British Championship in 1971, and his second in 1973. At the Isle of Man Rutter finished second to Agostini's MV Agusta in the 1972 Junior TT, but won in 1973 and 1974. A brief and bitter flirtation with John Player Norton Commandos during 1972 soured his impression of four-strokes until 1977, when he joined Honda-Britain to contest the Coupe d'Endurance. This led to a ride with the privateer Mocheck Honda team in 1978, Rutter coming close to beating the works Hondas in the British Formula One series until he crashed badly at the Island, breaking his leg. 1979 saw him back on a Formula One Honda. His first connection with Ducati was in 1980 after the Mocheck Honda was withdrawn from the TT. Rutter approached Sports Motorcycles, who hastily cobbled together a 900 bevel-drive racer for him, but it expired after one lap. However, this was the start of one of the most successful partnerships in racing and Rutter continued to improve. In 1982, now 40 years old, he also won the Junior TT on a Yamaha TZ350.

Tony Rutter's racing career tragically ended on 13 July 1985. Riding a TT1 Ducati in the Formula 1 race at Montjuich, the 44-year-old Rutter was involved in a seven-bike pile up. Rutter broke his neck in two places, but amazingly he survived. Despite not completing the season, Rutter still managed to finish second in the 1985 World TT Formula 2 Championship. To this day he remains the only Ducati rider to win four consecutive World Championships.

Tony Rutter with the factory TT2 at the start of the 1982 Isle of Man F2 TT. With him are factory mechanics Giuliano Pedretti (right) and Giovanni Mariannini. (Mick Woollett)

100 DUCATI RACERS

Club raffle provided financial support. The Pantah frame was sent to Ron Williams of Maxton for additional bracing, and to improve the steering Wynne fitted upright Koni shock absorbers and 900 SS fork triple clamps with 35mm racing Marzocchi forks. The wheels were Dymag 18-inch with Lockheed 260mm front discs, while the engine received 81mm 10:1 Omega pistons with cut down 750 liners. With 36mm Lectron carburettors, the 583cc Pantah pulled 145mph (233kmh) at 9,000rpm. Wynne fitted 900 NCR bodywork and Rutter easily won the 1981 F2 TT at an average speed of 101.91mph (163.97kmh), with a fastest lap of 103.51mph (166.58kmh). With only two rounds in the TT World Championship, Ducati then sent Franco Farnè and two TT2 factory machines (with 36mm carburettors as required by TT regulations, and a wet clutch) for Rutter at Ulster on 22 August. After setting the fastest lap in practice Rutter finished second in the wet conditions to secure the 1981 World TT Formula 2 Championship.

1982

For the defence of the Italian TT2 title, the factory TT2 received larger Dell'Orto PHM 41mm carburettors with short bell mouths, increasing the power slightly to 78bhp at 10,500rpm. The oil cooling system was upgraded to full flow cooling and chassis developments included the 280mm front brakes and a 16-inch Campagnolo front wheel with wider forks on some machines. During 1982, 20 catalogue TT2s were also produced. These were close in specification to the factory bikes, with a straight-cut primary drive and lightened crankshaft. Instead of the factory dry clutch with magnesium cover, the catalogue TT2 featured a larger riveted steel clutch basket for the wet multi-plate clutch. The gearbox was also stock but for a closer fifth gear. Similar to the factory machines were the 81mm Borgo pistons and 41mm and 35mm valves, but there were specific camshafts for the production TT2 providing 11mm of intake and 10.5mm of exhaust valve lift. Dell'Orto 36mm carburettors were fitted on the 1982 versions and with a two-into-one exhaust the power was 76bhp at 10,500rpm. The oil cooling system was identical to that on the 1981 factory version. These catalogue TT2s also came in a chassis similar to the factory racer. The Verlicchi frame was similar, as were the racing Marzocchi 35mm magnesium forks. The rear shock absorber was a Marzocchi PVS 1 remote reservoir type, and the wheels Campagnolo 2.15 and 2.50 x 18-inch. The front brakes were fully floating 280mm Brembo on the front, with a solid 260mm disc on the rear.

A year of development saw the TT2 even more successful in 1982. In the Junior Italian Formula 2 championship Walter Cussigh won all five rounds to take out the title. Cussigh favoured a 3.50 x 16-inch front and 3.50 x 18-inch rear wheel with larger section Michelin tyres. But it was in the three-round World TT Formula 2 Championship that the TT2, in the hands of Tony Rutter, proved its outstanding ability. At the end of May there was still some doubt as to when the promised factory TT2s would arrive, but two machines and mechanics (Giuliano Pedretti and Giovanni Mariannini) eventually turned up at the Isle of Man. Though these bikes were based on the catalogue TT2 with a wet clutch and 18-inch wheels, Rutter was immediately considerably quicker than the previous year. He convincingly won the Formula 2 race at an average speed of 108.50mph (174.61kmh), with a fastest lap of 109.27mph (175.85kmh), and was timed at 144mph (232kmh) at a speed trap at the Highlander. With the World Championship extended to three rounds, Rutter went to Vila Real in Portugal in July, where he won at an average speed of 86.69mph (139.51kmh) and Ducatis filled the first four places. Although he had already sewn up the title, Rutter went on to win the third round at Dunrod in Ulster at 100.73mph (162.1kmh).

The 1982 TT2 had an oil cooler takeoff to the cylinder head only, and all catalogue TT2s came with a wet clutch. Externally, the engine of Rutter's TT2 looked remarkably factory-standard. *(Roy Kidney)*

The TT2 was one of Ducati's finest limited production catalogue racers. Tony Rutter gave the TT2 its most success, although he generally raced with an 18-inch front wheel rather than the 16-inch here. *(Roy Kidney)*

Rutter's 1982 TT2 was a factory-prepared catalogue racer, lacking many of the special components of the Italian Championship machines. *(Roy Kidney)*

1983

The success of the TT2 during 1982 prompted the release of 30 more catalogue TT2 racers. Ostensibly identical to those of the previous year, the 1983 version included some of the features of Cussigh's 1982 factory machine. There were Dell'Orto 41mm carburettors, a revised full-flow oil cooling system, and 3.50 x 16-inch front and 3.50 x 18-inch rear Campagnolo wheels. The claimed power was 78bhp at 10,500rpm. Rutter was provided with a factory-prepared production TT2 for the TT Formula 2 World Championship, preferring an 18-inch front wheel on the bumpy road circuit. Expecting to dominate at the Isle of Man again, Graeme McGregor on a Sports Motorcycles Harris-framed TT2 led for the first two laps before succumbing to rear tyre problems. Rutter then took the lead and wasn't passed, setting a new lap record of 109.44mph (176.13kmh) although at 108.20mph (174.13kmh) his race average was slightly slower than the previous year. At the next round at Ulster, Rutter came second (although he set the fastest lap), repeating this at the final race at Assen in September. It was enough to give him a third straight title. McGregor may have lost the TT, but he had consolation in winning the British ACU TT F2 Championship on his Sports Motorcycles Harris TT2. In Italy, too, the TT2 continued to dominate this class of racing, Cussigh again winning the Junior Italian TT2 Championship.

1984

With a severe production crisis unfolding at Ducati during 1984, everything was scaled down, including the racing programme. Racing was undertaken by the 'Experimental Department', and apart from supporting Tony Rutter in the World Championship there were no longer any factory TT2s. With the emphasis on developing the endurance TT1, in the Junior Italian TT2 Championship it was left to NCR and GPM (Pietro di Gianesin) to uphold the TT2's impeccable record in this series, and this Fabio Barchitta did on the GPM TT2, narrowly winning from Luciano Leandrini (also TT2 mounted).

Tony Rutter now set up his own racing team, with Pat Slinn preparing the machines, and received an updated factory TT2. Changes in the regulations allowed 41mm Dell'Orto carburettors, and with 42 and 37mm valves the power was 81bhp at 10,200rpm. Similar to the factory 1983 TT2, Rutter's bike had magnesium engine covers and a dry clutch, with a Marzocchi Pulsar shock absorber. Rutter still preferred 18-inch wheels but could only manage second at the Isle of Man. Although reasonably happy with the new TT2 he considered it too heavy at 140kg (309lb) wet. He went on to win at Vila Real at 146.14kmh (90.83mph), take second at Ulster, and fifth at Brno, easily winning his fourth world title. Trevor Nation, on a Sports Motorcycles Harris TT2, came second in the championship.

Rutter ran his own team for 1984, with both a factory TT1 and TT2. Although he lost at the Isle of Man, he won the World TT Formula 2 Championship. This photo is autographed by Rutter. *(Author's Collection)*

1985

After testing the new factory TT1 at Imola towards the end of 1984, Rutter expected both a TT1 and TT2 for the 1985 season. However, Ducati arrived late at the Isle of Man, missing the early practice sessions, and bringing only a TT2. This was essentially a factory TT1 with a 600cc engine, and featured all the latest chassis updates, including 16-inch wheels, a braced aluminium swingarm with rising rate rear suspension, 42mm Marzocchi forks, and 300mm front discs with Brembo four-piston calipers. Although Rutter had described the 750 TT1 after testing as 'the best bike he'd ridden in 20 years and worth 40 seconds a lap round the Isle of Man,' after his first ride on the new TT2 he described the handling as 'diabolical.' However, by race day he was reasonably satisfied and won his fourth TT F2 race in five years, albeit at a slower speed of 107.79mph (173.47kmh). Despite its more sophisticated chassis, the new TT2 was not as stable on the bumps along the Sulby straight as the earlier version. Rutter then took the TT2 to second at Vila Real, and third at Montjuich before he crashed in the TT F1 race. Despite missing the final round Rutter still finished second in the World TT F2 Championship. By 1985 the two-stroke competition was too strong, and much of the success of the TT2 was undoubtedly due to outstanding ability of Tony Rutter, particularly at the Isle of Man. Graeme McGregor gave the TT2 one more World Championship victory, at Jerez in Spain in July 1986. With the demise of the World TT2 Championship, it was a fitting way for the magnificent TT2 to bow out.

THE 750 TT1

Historically all Ducati engines were designed with future capacity enlargement in mind and from the outset Taglioni had conceived the Pantah as a 750. Within a year the TT2 was stretched to a 750, Reno Leoni preparing a 750 for Jimmy Adamo in the 1982 Daytona 200, where he finished 13th. This produced nearly 95bhp at 10,250rpm, and had a top speed of almost 155mph (250kmh). The first official factory 750 appeared on 15 May 1982 at the Bol d'Or d'Italia 24 Hour endurance race at Imola. Ostensibly an experimental TT2 with an 88 x 61.5mm engine, this produced 92bhp and weighed 135kg (298lb). It was fitted with a 16-inch front wheel and new four-piston Brembo front brake calipers. Under the supervision of Taglioni and ridden by Mauro Ricci, Cussigh, and Filippo Suzzi, the 750 led in the first hour and was surprisingly competitive, but retired on lap 231 due to minor tyre and refuelling difficulties.

1983

All this was a prelude to a more concerted effort with the 750 TT1 during 1983. Tony Rutter had a factory 750cc engine at Daytona, and with this installed in his TT2 chassis he finished third in the Battle of the Twins race. He also managed a creditable 22nd in the 200 miler behind a field of works unlimited machinery. Then in July 1983, at Montjuich Park, a factory TT1 won the non-championship 24 Hour race in the hands of Benjamin Grau, Enrique de Juan, and Luis Reyes. Under the direction of Franco Farnè, the 135kg (298lb) racer produced 86bhp at 9,000rpm, but the riders limited this to 83–84bhp at 8,000rpm during the race. It ran an 18-inch front wheel and Marzocchi suspension. There was no Japanese competition at Montjuich, but a week later at Jarama the same machine was up to third in the Eight Hour race in a field of Kawasaki and Suzuki 1,000cc juggernauts. Not only was this a promising performance, but Cussigh and Oscar La Ferla raced the TT1 in the 1983 Senior Italian TT1 Championship. La Ferla won the first round at Misano in June, and Cussigh the final race at Vallelunga, Cussigh finishing second overall.

1984

As both TT1 and the Endurance World Championship were now restricted to 750cc, Ducati concentrated on development of the TT1 for 1984. A 61.5mm stroke was homologated through the 650SL Pantah, and two factory TT1s appeared at the Le Mans 24 Hour race on 22 April. There were two new TT1s for 1984. One was similar to the 1983 version but with a lighter frame, and a wider box-section aluminium swingarm (still with cantilever rear suspension). The wheels were 18-inch, the front brakes four-piston Brembo, and the Bosch ignition

Oscar La Ferla rode a TT1 to victory at Misano in June 1983. *(Author's Collection)*

Opposite: A small number of catalogue TT1s were also available during 1984, but these were ostensibly based on the TT2. *(Ian Falloon)*

Like the factory TT2, the TT1 endurance machines featured special dry clutch assemblies and a magnesium primary drive cover. This is Villa's 1984 machine. *(Author's Collection)*

was run dry with an exposed rotor on the left. Although the riders complained of poor handling, Marc Granie, Philippe Guichon, and Didier Vuillemin finished fourth.

The chief test rider for 1984 was former 250 and 350 World Champion Walter Villa. He had a machine with a new swingarm with rising rate suspension and was up to sixth at Le Mans before a gearbox failure ended his race. Villa's factory racer suffered from handling, piston, and valve seat problems all season, and the best result was his and Cussigh's fourth at the ADAC Eight Hour race at the Nürburgring. Granie and Guichon had more success. With a cantilever rear suspension, but a wider swingarm to accommodate the 16-inch wheels, they finished fourth at Österreichring, third in the Liège 24 Hours at Spa, and fourth at Mugello. Granie and Guichon ended ninth in the Endurance World Championship.

With 44 and 38mm valves, and camshafts providing intake lift of 11.45mm and exhaust lift 10.35mm, the 1984 750 endurance racer produced 87bhp at 10,000rpm at the rear wheel. There were Dell'Orto PHM 41 carburettors, and the Mahle pistons provided a 10.3:1 compression ratio. The con-rods were

RACING PANTAHS 107

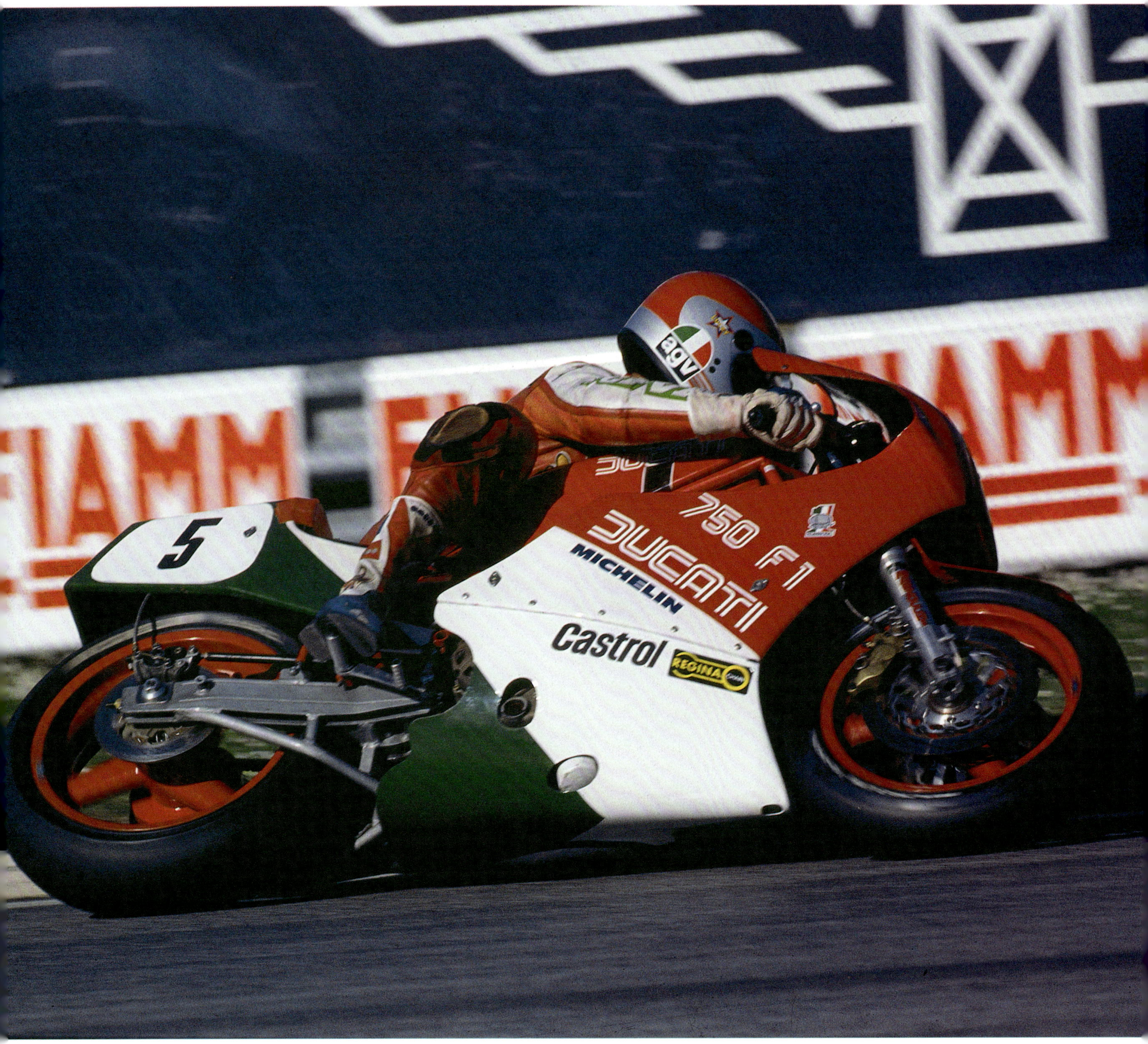
FIAMM
FIAMM
5
agv
750 F1
DUCATI
MICHELIN
Castrol
REGINA

Carrillo and there was a smaller 200-watt alternator. With magnesium outer engine covers the engine weighed 60kg (135lb). There was also a totally revised chassis. The Verlicchi box-section aluminium swingarm incorporated a rising rate linkage for the near vertical shock absorber. Ducati now built the frame, out of Columbus chrome-molybdenum tubing, with the steering head angle reduced to 24°. During the season experimentation with Marvic wheels included a 16-inch front wheel, with either a 16, 17 or 18-inch rear. The rear rim width went up to 5.5in (140mm) to accommodate new Michelin radial tyres. Also tried were 41.7mm Kayaba (with hydraulic anti-dive), similar 42mm Marzocchi forks, and a Marzocchi, White Power or Double System of Rome type. The front brakes were Brembo fully floating 300mm with four-piston calipers and the rear a 230mm, and riding on a 1,370mm wheelbase (4ft 5.9in) the weight was 130kg (287lb).

For 1984 a catalogue TT1 was also available. This was more closely related to the TT2 than the factory TT1 as it retained the Verlicchi frame with cantilever swingarm. The engine had 41 and 35mm valves, a hydraulic wet clutch, and with 41mm carburettors produced 80bhp at the rear wheel. The aluminium swingarm was wider than the TT2, to accommodate a wider rear wheel, with the countershaft sprocket offset. The rear wheel now included an endurance-style quick-change assembly. The wheels were 16 and 18-inch, similar to the TT2, as were the 35mm magnesium Marzocchi forks and 280mm Brembo front discs with 05 calipers. These catalogue TT1s were very competitive racers. Grau, Reyes, and Garriga took one to victory in the 1984 Barcelona 24 Hour race on 14 July. Tony Rutter rode his to third at the Isle of Man, consistent results seeing him third overall in the World TT Formula 1 Championship. Rutter also won the European Battle of the Twins Series on the TT1.

1985

With even more financial restraint required regarding racing development for the 1985 season, there were only a few changes to the 750 endurance racer and factory TT1 machines. Already the 750 had proven competi-

Opposite: The 1985 factory TT1 was a beautiful and highly effective racing machine. Marco Lucchinelli rode to victory at Imola in April. *(Author's Collection)*

On a similar machine Virginio Ferrari took out the 1985 Italian TT F1 Championship. Later in the season there were new Marzocchi M1R forks. *(Museo Ducati)*

tive, but reliability had been questionable during 1984. After some Mahle piston failure, there was a return to two-ring Borgo pistons. The exhaust valve went up to 40mm, and with Dell'Orto 42mm carburettors the power was 92bhp at 10,000rpm at the rear wheel. There were new Marzocchi M1R forks too, and along with improved reliability the 1985 endurance racer weighed less, at 122kg (269lb).

An injection of funds from Cagiva following its purchase of the Ducati company (see next chapter) allowed for an increase in the racing programme for 1985. As well as the Endurance World Championship there were several TT1s entered in the Italian Formula One Championship. Dieter Rechtenbach also received a factory TT1 for the German and World TT F1 series. The season started with Marco Lucchinelli riding a Leoni-prepared TT1 in both the Daytona 100 Formula 1 and the Battle of the Twins races. He acquitted himself well, with a sixth in the F1 and second in the Twins. In the Endurance World Championship the only finish was at Monza in June, where Cussigh and La Ferla came fifth, with Virginio Ferrari and Lucchinelli sixth. However, it was a different story in Italian F1. Ferrari won the championship from Lucchinelli, TT1s filling out the top seven places. After not receiving a TT1 for the Isle of Man, Rutter had one for Vila Real, where he came fifth, and Montjuich, where he crashed. In the World TT Formula 1 Championship Dieter Rechtenbach managed sixth overall, with his best result a second at Montjuich. Again the TT1 triumphed at the Montjuich endurance race, Grau, de Juan, and Garriga this time riding a Tecfar-TT1 with an Antonio Cobas chassis.

1986–87

After the disappointing endurance results of 1985 Ducati's new owners Cagiva decided to concentrate on events that were more suited to the ageing Pantah. At the 1986 Daytona meeting there was a team of five factory machines, along with an imposing entourage that included Taglioni, Farnè, and Pedretti. For the Battle of the Twins race there were two TT1s with rising rate rear suspension, Lucchinelli having an experimental TT1 with an 851cc (92 x 64mm) 97bhp

Although Lucchinelli won the 1986 Battle of the Twins race on an 851cc TT1, he also raced this 750 F1 Superbike.
(Museo Ducati)

engine, and Adamo a similar 818cc (92 x 61.5mm) machine. Stefano Caracchi had the Spanish Tecfar-Cobas machine, and there were two 750 F1-based racers for the Superbike race.

Former World 500cc Champion Marco Lucchinelli had a very good year with the TT1 during 1986. In the Daytona Battle of the Twins race he sped away to victory at more than 104mph (167kmh), Adamo crashing on the banking while dicing for second. Lucchinelli also qualified the 750F1 for the Superbike event, but retired in the race. He then went to the opening round of the World TT Formula 1 Championship on 6 April, originally billed as the Imola 200 but rescheduled at Misano. Lucchinelli led for most of the race, winning at an average speed of 90.14mph (145kmh). He returned to the US in July with the 851 TT1, winning the BOTT race at Laguna Seca. After the debut of the new Desmoquattro 748 at the Bol d'Or, Lucchinelli teamed with Garriga on a 750 TT1 at the World Championship Jerez Eight Hour race on 28 September. They had pole position and initially led the race, finishing second to the works Honda of Igoa and Vieira. The next month, at the non-championship Barcelona 24 Hour race, Grau, Garriga, and Carlos Cardus won on the 851cc TT1.

These impressive performances provided the impetus for Taglioni to continue development of the Pantah. The final TT1 racer appeared early in 1987. Cagiva GP rider Raymond Roche tested it at Misano in April, and Lucchinelli raced it at Laguna Seca. This 851 TT1 featured revised inlet ports, long air ducts, and metal shrouding around the rear cylinder. There were 43mm upside-down GCB (Gazzaniga-Ceriani-Bianchi) forks with a single central spring and gas-pressurised shock absorber. At the rear was a GCB rear shock absorber and the wheels were Marvic 17-inch front and rear. In the hands of Lucchinelli, this final incarnation of the TT1 was good enough to win the Pro Twins Grand Prix at Laguna Seca in July 1987. This was the final victory for the TT1 but already there were few categories left for it. With the demise of the World TT Formula 1 Championship and the ascendancy of Superbike there was even less of a future for an air-cooled two-valve twin. By 1988 even Fabio Taglioni had to concede the road racing days of the Pantah were over.

PARIS–DAKAR

Although the Pantah was outclassed in road racing by 1987, it had an afterlife in off-road racing. Soon after Cagiva had entered into an agreement with Ducati in 1983 to supply Pantah engines, they announced their off-road Elefant. Giampaolo Marinoni debuted the Elefant in Morocco in 1984, and a factory machine was prepared for the 1985 Paris–Dakar race. Based on the 650 Elefant, this displaced 750cc, and with 9:1 compression and 36mm Dell'Orto carburettors the power was 80bhp. Suspension was by twin Öhlins rear shock absorbers, with a Marzocchi fork, and weight was 160kg (353lb) dry. After crashing while in the lead, Hubert Auriol rode to seventh. Later that year he finished fourth in the Pharaoh's Rally.

For the 1986 race the Elefant displaced 850cc (92 x 64mm), and with 40mm Dell'Orto carburettors produced 83bhp. There was longer travel Marzocchi suspension but the weight was up to 180kg (397lb). It was a tragic race for Cagiva as their rider Marinoni died following a crash. Auriol and 'Ciro' De Petri rode the 850 Elefants in the 1987 Paris–Dakar rally. Now with a Paso-derived engine with a Weber carburettor, and a new chassis with a rising-rate linkage rear suspension, Auriol looked set to win until he had an accident towards the end of the race. De Petri then won the Pharaoh's Rally, but crashed in the 1988 Paris–Dakar. This year the Elefant displaced 904cc (92 x 68mm), and with a Weber DCNF36 carburettor produced 85bhp. De Petri won the Tunisia Rally in 1988 but it wasn't until 1990 that the Cagiva Elefant fulfilled its expectations. Now with an air and oil cooled 944cc (94 x 68mm) engine with Mikuni CV carburettors prepared by the Ducati racing department, Edi Orioli finally won the Paris–Dakar rally. De Petri came third on a 904cc version, the Cagivas winning nine of the 17 legs.

Former 250cc World Motocross Champion Danny LaPorte joined the Cagiva team for 1991, winning the Pharaoh's Rally and coming second in the 1992 Paris–Cape Town rally on the 944 Elefant. Orioli was back for 1993, winning the Pharaoh's, and providing Cagiva with their second Paris–Dakar victory in 1994. In 1995 Jodi Arcarons finished second in the Granada–Dakar Rally, with Orioli third. For nearly a decade the Pantah engine had proved extremely reliable and eminently suited to this demanding form of competition.

Arcarons on his way to second in the 1995 Granada–Dakar Rally. (Author's Collection)

During the early 1990s the Cagiva Elefant was a formidable competitor in the Paris–Dakar and similar events. This is Arcarons again in 1995. (Author's collection)

★ Lucky
618
4valves DOHC
DUCATI
DESMO
WEBER
brembo
MICHELIN
MARZOCCHI
REGINA CHAIN
DOUBLE SYSTEM

7 NEW GENERATION

Compared to the final TT1s the 851 looked big and overweight, but even in its early days of development it was incredibly fast.

(Cycle World)

Following the uncertainty of the early 1980s under the control of Finmeccanica and the VM Group, the purchase of Ducati by Cagiva in 1985 heralded a new era. A burgeoning motorcycle manufacturer owned by the Castiglioni brothers, Claudio and Gianfranco, Cagiva was based in the northern Italian city of Varese. During 1985 motorcycle production at the Borgo Panigale plant numbered only 1,924, but by 1986 Cagiva had increased this to 5,979. However, Cagiva's priority wasn't only to increase production. They also wanted to race, and even though the Pantah-based racers were providing satisfactory results in BOTT, the Castiglioni brothers considered that the future lay in Superbike racing. They were also sufficiently far-sighted to sanction the development of an engine embracing up-to-date thermodynamic and engine management technology.

Fabio Taglioni's distrust of four-valves per cylinder was legendary. His experience with them was disappointing. Because of the shape of the intake ports, both the 1971 Grand Prix 500cc bevel-drive four-valve and subsequent belt-drive Armaroli design of 1973 offered little improvement over existing two-valve designs. He also remembered the ill-fated 125 four, and the failure of the Ricardo 350 Triple further accentuated his mistrust. Taglioni did have a pair of four-valve heads cast for the 900 Super Sport in 1978 but he never bench-tested them. He was also suspicious of water-cooling and favoured smaller, lighter, and less complicated machinery. He had plans for a V-four – virtually two 500cc Pantah engines side-by-side – but this was shelved at the end of 1982.

The Castiglionis could have resurrected Taglioni's V-four, but instead they chose a different path. They preferred a four-valve twin based on the existing Pantah and engaged Massimo Bordi to coordinate the project. Bordi came to Ducati in 1978 with an engineering thesis on an air-cooled four-valve desmodromic cylinder head, completed in 1975 under the supervision of Taglioni and Professor Bartolozzi at Bologna University. Bordi was enthusiastic about implementing modern technology and was an admirer of Cosworth, known for their successful Formula One racing car engines. Bordi was at Cosworth from September 1985 until January 1986, and they offered to develop and produce a prototype non-desmodromic engine. Considered too expensive by the Castiglionis, they entrusted the design to Bordi instead, who initially considered four, five, and six valve heads with conventional valve springs. As the Castiglionis wanted to maintain a desmodromic valve system he finally decided on a four-valve desmo.

THE 748

In early 1986 Gianluigi 'Gigi' Mengoli began drawing a liquid-cooled double overhead camshaft four-valve desmodromic cylinder head that could be adapted to Pantah crankcases. 'I had to work at home in the evenings to avoid the wrath of Taglioni, who was still sceptical of the new engine,' says Mengoli, who had the drawings finished by 13 April. It was significant that the cylinder head was designed for racing rather than low cost and featured a 40° included valve angle, from the Cosworth F2 FVA 1,600cc engine. Unlike Bordi's earlier thesis with the four rockers positioned outside the camshafts, all the rockers were located between them. With this desmodromic rocker set-up a narrower included valve angle was impossible. Cosworth also helped design a suitable exhaust and injection system, allowing a straight inlet manifold with a 45° downdraft and 48mm throttle bodies. The new liquid-cooled engine also featured Pantah-style toothed rubber belts to drive the double overhead camshafts. The valve sizes on the prototype were 34mm inlet, and 30mm exhaust, with an 11.0:1 compression ratio, still with a flat-topped Mondial piston and Tecnol cylinders. The con-rods were Carrillo, with the same 124mm (4.9in) length as the Pantah and a 20mm gudgeon.

Almost as important as the cylinder head design was incorporation of the Weber Marelli 'IAW Alfa/N' open-loop fully-mapped electronic fuel injection system, originally developed for the Ferrari F40 sports car and Formula One. The computer used an EPROM (electronically programmable read only memory) that contained a map of fuel and ignition requirements derived from dyno tests. Work on adapting this system to a motorcycle began in January 1986 under the leadership of Aurelia Lionello. His team at Marelli (Busi, Mezzette, and Lenzi) soon found that electronic fuel injection gave an important volumetric efficiency advantage and was particularly suited to twin-cylinder engines.

Using modified Pantah crankcases (with more widely spaced cylinder studs), the prototype engine was 748cc so it could run in the Bol d'Or 24 Hour endurance race at Paul Ricard in the south of France on 19 September 1986. The dimensions of 88 x 61.5mm came from the 750 TT1, and in determining the size of the cooling system Bordi used his earlier experience with diesel engines. A water pump was fitted on the left, running off the cam belt drive shaft, moving the water through a 14 pass cross-flow radiator. It wasn't the neatest arrangement but was indicative of the urgency of completion. In April 1986 the blueprint drawings were dispatched to the foundry and work proceeded, continuing thereafter until the engine was first started on 30 August. The first time on the dyno this produced 82.18bhp at 7,862rpm, soon rising to 94bhp. To speed development the engine was placed in a modified TT1 frame that had been prepared during the August summer break. This was a traditional tubular steel space frame (with 25 x 1.5mm main tubing) and a braced aluminium swingarm, also featuring a linkage rising rate rear suspension with a GSG Double System shock absorber. To reduce some of the coolant plumbing the 22mm triangular cross tube was incorporated as a coolant pipe. By 15 September the 170kg (375lb)

Gianluigi Mengoli with the 748 at the Bol d'Or. Mengoli joined Ducati in 1973 and is the current head of the technical department.
(Gianluigi Mengoli)

Hastily constructed, the 748 wasn't the most beautiful racer, but it was promising and paved the way for the future.
(Gianluigi Mengoli)

NEW GENERATION **115**

Lucchinelli's Daytona 1987 851 was a development of the Bol d'Or 748, and still very much a prototype. *(Cycle World)*

748 was ready for its first test at Mugello, and at the Bol d'Or was ridden by Marco Lucchinelli, Juan Garriga, and Virginio Ferrari. The 748 was in seventh place after 13 hours before retiring with a broken con-rod bolt.

This retirement almost saw an end to the four-valve project. The two-valve 851cc TT1 had reached a stage where it was fast and reliable and Taglioni wanted to persevere with its development. Bordi, though, was still committed to the four-valve project and by early 1987 had also increased the capacity to 851cc (92 x 64mm). The four-valve immediately proved more powerful than the two-valve, and with 115bhp it was the first time a Ducati engine had exceeded the 100bhp mark.

THE 851

Early in 1987 Bordi and Mengoli designed new crankcases for the 851. Stronger, and allowing for a six-speed gearbox, the deeper sump provided half a litre more oil with full length mounting bosses across the crankcase. The valve sizes were reduced to 32mm for the inlet, with 10mm of valve lift, and 28mm for the exhaust, with 9mm of lift. The reduction in valve sizes was in response to Ferrari's experience with the 312T flat-12 F1 car engine, where it was found that small valves combined with an extreme bore/stroke ratio improved mid-range power. Three-ring Mondial pistons provided a 12:1 compression ratio, and the crankshaft and 124mm (4.9in) forged con-rods were highly polished. The Weber Marelli injection system was much as before, with twin injectors per cylinder and 47mm throttle bodies, and the power was 120bhp at 11,500rpm at the rear wheel. There was little attempt made to improve the engine aesthetics and the power unit was still dominated by a maze of pipes and wires.

The chassis was similar to the Bol d'Or 748 prototype. There was a 27° steering head angle, 42mm Marzocchi M1R forks, a GSG Roma Double System single shock absorber, and 17-inch Marvic wheels. The front Brembo brakes were twin 320mm floating discs with four-piston calipers, with a 230mm disc at the rear. The weight was also slightly less at 165kg (364lb), and the wheelbase a moderate 1,430mm (4ft 8.3in). With its bodywork based on the 748, the 851 was also no beauty, but it was effective.

In March 1987 the 851 was entered in the Daytona the Battle of the Twins race. Lucchinelli won easily, and was timed at 165.44mph (266.19kmh), only 6mph (9.7kmh) down on Wayne Rainey's factory Honda VFR 750 Superbike. It was such an impressive performance that Lucchinelli then contested the 1987 Italian Superbike Trophy, pitting 1,000cc twins against 750cc fours. Here the lack of development immediately became evident. Reliability suffered as revs increased and crankshafts failed. There were also consistent electrical problems caused through vibration, and the engine would sometimes inexplicably stall. According to Massimo Bordi 'it took a complete season to isolate a

When Lucchinelli gave the 851 its first victory at Daytona in 1987 there was no turning back for the Desmoquattro. (Museo Ducati)

To homologate the 851 for World Superbike racing Ducati released the 851 Superbike Kit in 1988. Complete with headlight and tail light this was overweight and uncompetitive. *(Australian Motorcycle News)*

Lucchinelli gave the 851 a dream debut in the first ever World Superbike race at Donington in 1988. Here he leads future Ducati Corse team manager Davide Tardozzi on a Bimota YB4EI. *(Australian Motorcycle News)*

problem caused by the flywheel pick-ups failing in the extreme oil temperatures.' These engine management malfunctions eventually led to Marelli modifying the software during 1989.

Because of these problems Lucchinelli only won two Italian Superbike races during 1987, at Monza and Misano. Consistent engine development throughout the season saw new Tecno Cereal cylinders substituted and the valve sizes going back to 34 and 30mm. To prevent further crankshaft failure Austrian Pankl titanium con-rods (H-section in the style of a Carrillo) with larger (42mm, up from 40mm) big-end journals replaced the Pantah type. Chassis development during 1987 also saw a reduction in the steering head angle to 26°.

The year 1988 saw the establishment of the World Superbike Championship, and here was another series that seemed ideally suited to the new 851. Not only were twins allowed to displace 1,000cc, but their minimum weight limit was only 140kg (309lb), compared to the 750cc fours' 165kg (364lb). Also, as a manufacturer producing less than 50,000 motorcycles a year the homologation requirements for World Superbike were just 200 units. Ducati's homologation machine was the 851 Superbike Kit, and 207 were produced in January 1988. A confused amalgam of racer and street bike, this came with Michelin slick racing tyres, but also an electric start, headlight, and tail-light.

Inside the engine were 32 and 28mm nimonic valves, and desmodromic 'kit' camshafts. The 92mm piston gave a compression ratio of 10.7:1, and there were Pankl con-rods and a close ratio six-speed 'kit' gearbox. The Weber Marelli electronic ignition and fuel injection system was also the same P7 system of the factory racer, with twin injectors per cylinder and two pick-ups. The 851cc engine produced a claimed 120bhp at 10,000rpm at the crankshaft, but this wasn't sufficient to make the 851 Superbike Kit a competitive Superbike racer.

The Superbike Kit chassis was based on the 1987 factory racer, the chrome-molybdenum tubular steel frame featuring a 27° steering head angle. There was a braced aluminium swingarm with rising rate linkage and Marzocchi 41.7mm M1R forks and a Supermono rear shock absorber. The wheels were magnesium Marvic 3.50 and 5.50 x 17-inch, and the front brakes 280mm fully floating cast-iron Brembo with P4.32B calipers (with four 32mm pistons). At the rear was a 260mm disc.

Apart from a confused identity and little information on the injection system, the Superbike Kit's main problem was the weight. Although claimed to weigh 165kg (364lb) this was extremely optimistic, and the Kit was extremely uncompetitive as a privateer Superbike racer. However, with factory assistance it was suitable for BOTT. Stefano Caracchi brought a factory 851 Superbike Kit to Daytona in 1988, where he finished second in the Pro-Twins race. The machine was then further developed by Eraldo Ferracci, and in the hands of Dale Quarterley won the Pro-Twins title. In Italy, Baldassare Monti won the Italian Twins Championship, earning him a ride in the World Superbike squad for the next season.

WORLD SUPERBIKE 1988

Although the 851 disappointed in the 1987 Italian Superbike Trophy, Ducati was undeterred and decided to contest the new World Superbike Championship. Their confidence was rewarded, and at the first World Superbike race at Donington on 3 April 1988, Marco Lucchinelli took an overall victory. His second in the first leg and a win in the second continued the Ducati tradition of debut victories. Although Lucchinelli also won the first race at Zeltweg in Austria, electrical and crankshaft problems resulted in subsequent retirements, just as had happened during 1987. Experimentation with induction and exhaust systems, 11.2:1 Mondial pistons, and 33 and 29mm valves, saw the power of the 851 rise to 122bhp at 11,000rpm. The throttle bodies were now 50mm, and after Austria 94mm pistons increased the capacity to 888cc. As the power increased, problems surfaced with the main bearings, lubrication, and crankcases.

During the season there was continual development to the chassis. There were different swingarms, experimental 42mm Marzocchi upside-down forks, and a reduction in the steering head angle to 24°.

During 1988 the 851 was continually developed but was unreliable. By the end of the season it featured a heavily braced swingarm and upside-down Marzocchi forks. (Author's Collection)

Opposite: In his first season on the 888 Raymond Roche was frustrated by mechanical and electrical problems, but found it impressively fast. (Phil Aynsley)

Although he wasn't officially retired from racing, Marco Lucchinelli became team manager for Squadra Corse in 1989. (Author's Collection)

However, getting near the minimum weight of 140kg (309lb) was difficult, and the 1988 factory racer still weighed in at 162kg (357lb). Citing budget problems, Ducati decided not to contest the final two World Superbike rounds in Australia and New Zealand, even though Lucchinelli was still in sight of the title and could have won, as his main rival Davide Tardozzi crashed out of both races. Instead he finished fifth overall.

1989

For the 1988 season Lucchinelli became Squadra Corse team manager. Raymond Roche was signed up as number one rider, along with Baldassare Monti. Massimo Broccoli and Lucchinelli also rode on occasion. Ducati again contested the Italian Superbike Championship, with Monti and Broccoli. With a displacement of 888cc, a new combustion chamber with 36 and 31mm valves, and a revised exhaust system, the power was up to 128bhp. Roche had a choice of three engine/gearbox combinations for each race. 'If the gearbox is not right

NEW GENERATION

for the track we cannot change it – you cannot change anything on this bike,' Roche said.

There was further emphasis on weight saving, and this was now down to 158kg (349lb). Suspension developments included 42mm upside-down Öhlins forks and a stronger swingarm. Unfortunately there were still too many mechanical and electrical problems and although Roche won five races he only ended third in the championship. At some of the fastest circuits (Hockenheim and Brainerd) he took double victories, indicating the impressive speed of the 888. Monti also salvaged some pride by giving the 851 success in the Italian Superbike Championship, its first series victory.

As the 851 Superbike Kit was proving uncompetitive, an official modification kit was released during 1989. This was quite comprehensive and indicated the factory was more serious about supporting privateer Superbike racers. Included were 94mm pistons and cylinders (giving 888cc), larger valves (33 and 29mm), a larger air intake, and new exhaust system, along with a corresponding EPROM kit of four replacements (up to five per cent richer). The compression ratio went up to 11.2:1 and the power at the crankshaft to 132bhp at 10,500rpm. To improve breathing the top of the airbox was lowered 30mm (1.18in) and the fuel tank raised 10mm (0.39in). Other components included a lighter (180-watt) alternator, aluminium timing pulleys, and lighter clutch and flywheel. Also included were the fastenings to fit the smaller (5-Ah) battery beside the engine rather than in the tail. New front and rear aluminium subframes positioned the ECU in front of the steering head. Other components deemed unnecessary included the electric start motor, timing belt covers, thermostat, electric fan, and headlight. There was also a lightweight fibreglass fairing kit. Improved chassis components included 300mm front discs and a new rear shock absorber. Some of these modification kits were factory-fitted to the 851 Superbike Kit, the result being the red 851 Racing, or 'Lucchinelli' Replica. But even with the modification kit there was a huge gulf between the official factory machines and those of the privateers. This had always been the case, but the mysteries of the Weber electronic fuel injection seemed to amplify the difference.

1990

Encouraged by the improved results of 1989, there was an expanded World Superbike effort for 1990. Giancarlo Falappa joined Roche in the team but soon earned a reputation for crashing, his season ending following a serious crash at the Österreichring in practice. Although Roche still wasn't totally happy with the 888 further development saw it the leading championship contender. Emphasis centred on improving reliability, but with the electronic troubles overcome the lubrication system and crankcases were now problematic. The inertia from the heavy Pankl con-rods deformed the pistons, unsealing the piston rings and causing excessive crankcase pressure. The crankcases also cracked around the main bearing bosses. The racing department was kept busy building replacement engines, and on a couple of occasions they failed spectacularly.

New injector trumpets improved airflow, and there were 12:1 pistons, but the combustion chamber shape still required 45° of ignition advance. The inlet valves were now up to 37mm, and with new camshafts the power was 130bhp at 11,000rpm at the rear wheel. There was a smaller, single curved radiator, raising the temperature to around 70–75°C after it was found that the engine had been running too cool during 1989 (40°C). Searching to improve combustion, later in the year there was a 920cc engine (with 95.6mm pistons) for faster circuits, but the 888cc version was considered more tractable.

The chassis was much as before, with similar Öhlins suspension and Brembo brakes. Lowering the ride height increased the steering head angle, and the rear section was stiffened with two additional struts. After starting the season at 157kg (346lb) the weight was gradually reduced to 150kg (331lb). An *evoluzione* machine appeared at Monza, with carbon fibre mufflers, tank, and fairing. There was new LCD instrumentation and the CPU (central processing unit) was moved from under the tailpiece to in front of the steering head. The weight was reduced even further, to 147kg (324lb).

Roche looked dominant from the outset, winning two opening races at Jerez. There was no doubt that the 888's weight advantage and more racing orientated

Development to the 888 for 1990 included new intake and cooling systems. *(Ian Falloon)*

Despite continual crankcase cracking problems, Roche gave Ducati their first World Superbike Championship in 1990. *(Ian Falloon)*

NEW GENERATION **123**

Following his retirement from racing, Raymond Roche became the Ducati racing team manager. This is his 1993 team of Giancarlo Falappa and Carl Fogarty. *(Author's Collection)*

RAYMOND ROCHE

When he joined the Squadra Corse Ducati team for 1989, Roche was already a seasoned veteran. Born in Ollioules in the south of France on 21 February 1957, Roche spent five years in 500 Grand Prix racing, with a best result of third on a Honda in the 1984 500cc World Championship. He also won the 1981 World Endurance Championship on a Kawasaki. Roche moved to Cagiva in 1987 and after a disappointing 1988 season it was only a small step to a factory Ducati in the World Superbike Championship. Roche's first year with Ducati was not the happiest. 'At first I thought I could win easily on the Ducati, but it failed six times. Although I won many races, set many lap records, many pole positions, I did not win the World Championship.'

Roche was obviously far happier with the motorcycle during 1990 as suspension and tyre improvements made it easier to ride. But he still felt there was room for improvement: 'I would like the engine to be shorter, maybe change the cylinder head, and then we can change the frame.' Roche's 1991 season was also difficult because there were now more factory Ducatis to contend with. Continually dogged by poor starts, Roche initially underestimated Doug Polen and had to work his way through the field to get decent results. For 1992 Roche elected not to ride for the factory team, but with tuner Rolando Simonetti often had the fastest bikes on the track. Before the season Roche had been told there would be no huge factory effort during 1992. He was therefore dismayed at the first round at Albacete when he turned up with his two bikes in a small van to see the huge Ducati race transporter in the paddock. This seemed to spur Roche on but he was penalised for his slow starts. 1992 was his final racing season and for 1993 he became yet another distinguished ex-factory rider to manage the World Superbike team.

---

design gave it an advantage. With eight victories Roche easily took the championship. Falappa won at Donington, and Jamie James's two second places at Mosport on the Fast by Ferracci 851 saw him on Falappa's bike for Sugo, Le Mans, and Monza. Although Roche won by 57 points, Ducati lost the Manufacturers' World Championship to Honda by six points.

There were also 20 Roche Replica 851 Racing machines for 1990. Essentially based on the 1989 888cc factory bike, these featured the new inlet camshaft (known as the 'G' cam) with 11mm of valve lift, a modified airbox, racing clutch and gearbox, and a magnesium clutch cover. The chassis was significantly improved over the Lucchinelli Replica, with Öhlins upside-down front forks. The Brembo 320mm front disc brakes featured updated four-piston calipers and at the rear was a 210mm disc. The claimed weight was 158kg (349lb). Although the Roche Replicas were more competitive than earlier over-the-counter 851s, without factory support they were still disappointing. It was only in Battle of the Twins Championships that they had any success, Jamie James winning the AMA Pro-Twins Championship and Danilo Toschi the Italian BOTT Championship.

1991

Determined to also win the constructors' championship, Doug Polen and Stéphane Mertens also received factory 888s for 1991. With Falappa still recovering from his crash the previous year Roche was the only rider in Lucchinelli's Squadra Corse team for the first few rounds. Not only were there more machines on the grid, but the 888 was much improved, and was only beaten once (by Kevin Magee on a Yamaha) during the season.

As crankcase failure was the most serious problem during 1990, there were new crankcases built out of a higher grade of aluminium from Alcan in Canada. There was also reinforcing around the main bearings to prevent cracking. The pistons were now British Omega (as used by Steve Wynne), providing a 13:1 compression ratio, and still with Mondial cylinders. The Pankl con-rods now featured an oil way drilled up the shaft to the little end and lubrication further improved by

Doug Polen showing the style that took him to the 1991 World Superbike Championship. He completely dominated on the Fast by Ferracci 888.
(Author's Collection)

locating the oil pump suction rose lower. More attention was also paid to reducing internal friction. The valve sizes were 36 and 31mm, the camshafts were unchanged, but a new combustion chamber shape saw a reduction in ignition advance to 40° at maximum rpm. The inlet ports were increased to 30mm, and there was a new exhaust system, with two separate pipes from each exhaust port all the way to the crossover. There were also developments to the airbox and induction chamber, and the power of the 888cc engine was 133bhp at 11,500rpm.

As with the *evoluzione* 888 that appeared at the end of the 1990 season, even more attention was paid to weight saving. Now weighing only 143kg (316lb), there was extensive use of carbon fibre for most brackets, while the repositioning of various components such as the computer improved weight distribution to 51/49 per cent. The factory bikes of Roche and Falappa also featured a steel/carbon front disc combination, a new Öhlins front fork, and a reduction in the rear disc size to 190mm (from 216mm). To improve the aerodynamics new bodywork was developed in the Pininfarina wind tunnel. This included a new front mudguard, higher mounted mufflers, and a rear guard running underneath the swingarm, and resulted in a five per cent improvement in wind penetration. No one was quite prepared when Polen won the opening round at Donington on the Fast by Ferracci 888. Polen (on Dunlop tyres) totally dominated the season. He won 17 races to Roche's four (on Michelin tyres), and Mertens's two (on Pirelli tyres), and Ducati easily won the Manufacturers' Championship.

Fifty examples of the 851 Racing were also produced for 1991. The compression ratio of the 888cc engine went up to 12:1, and although the valve sizes remained at 34 and 30mm the inlet ports were increased to 29mm. There was a new 20-plate clutch and a closer ratio gearbox became available during the year. Producing a claimed 128bhp at 11,000rpm, chassis developments included wider wheels (a 3.75 x 17 and 6.00 x 17-inch), Brembo P4 30/34 front brake calipers, and more carbon fibre, the weight being 155kg (342lb). Davide Tardozzi won the European Superbike Championship on one of these machines. There was also a half-heated return to endurance racing during 1991, but the endurance 888 proved unreliable.

After Carl Fogarty, the amiable Texan Doug Polen has been the most successful Ducati rider in the World Superbike Championship. *(Ian Falloon)*

DOUG POLEN

Working as a motorcycle mechanic, Doug Polen started racing in 1979. Born in Detroit, Michigan, on 2 September 1960, Polen was brought up in Texas and by 1981 had his expert's licence. He finished the season 19th in AMA Superbike Championship and was broke. In 1982 he quit racing to study computer science, but by 1986 was able to make a living racing in the Suzuki GSX-R series. He won almost every GSX-R race in the US, and a reputed $100,000, moving to Superbike and Supersport in 1987. By 1988 he was on a Yoshimura Suzuki and finished second in the AMA Superbike Championship. Lured by a bigger fee, Polen moved to Japan in 1989. Here he won the All Japan Formula One and Formula Three Championships on a Yoshimura Suzuki. Then, after losing some toes off his left foot after it became tangled in a Suzuki's rear wheel, Doug Polen decided it was time for a change. He looked to Ducati. 'I'd always been curious about Ducati as it was a completely different motorcycle to the Japanese bikes.'

Polen first tested the Fast by Ferracci 888 at Daytona at the end of November 1990, and then a week later rode Raymond Roche's 888 at an international Superbike race in Mexico. He won both races: 'It was the first time I had ridden a twin and my initial impressions were good.' After Polen set pole position at Daytona in 1991 on the Fast by Ferracci entry, but broke a drive chain on the start line, Eraldo Ferracci decided to attempt the year's World Superbike Championship. With the assistance of Giorgio Nepoti and Rino Caracchi of NCR, Polen and the Fast by Ferracci bike went on to set records that could last forever, including seven consecutive World Superbike victories and ten pole positions in a season. This secured Polen the championship, an achievement he repeated in 1992. Instead of returning to defend his World Superbike title a second time he stayed in the US during 1993 and gave Ducati their first AMA Superbike crown. Then he defected to Honda but couldn't come to terms with the RC45. Polen's final success was in the World Endurance Championship, winning this in 1997 on a Suzuki, and in 1998 on a Honda.

1992

Marco Lucchinelli's imprisonment for cocaine possession saw another former 500cc World Champion, Franco Uncini, as manager of the official Ducati team. Doug Polen now rode for Uncini, bringing Eraldo Ferracci as technical manager, and Falappa was resigned. Roche was also supplied factory bikes, and Stéphane Mertens, Davide Tardozzi, and Spanish rider Daniel Amatriain received factory equipment. The race department was kept very busy and 50 engines were prepared during the year.

Most of the development for 1992 was on the induction system. A still-air box was formed by the underside of the fuel tank and sealed by a carbon fibre shroud. The intakes were increased to 54mm and Roche had a variable length inlet bellmouth operated by a small power-valve like motor. There was also experimentation with double mapping, with each cylinder receiving an individual computer and EPROM. With 36 and 31mm valves, a new exhaust camshaft, a narrower crankpin, and smaller crank flywheels, the 888cc engine now revved to 12,000rpm. Completing the updates were a new clutch, stainless steel exhaust system, narrower (6mm rather than 10mm) gears, and hollow camshafts. Although the power of the 888cc engine was only increased marginally, to 135bhp at 11,200rpm, the power delivery was smoother. The engine also produced 109bhp at only 8,000rpm.

Although the 1992 production 888 featured a new frame, the racing models retained the 1991 type with individually welded top tubes and the earlier footpeg brackets. The carbon fibre bodywork was also patterned on the 1991 851 and not the 1992 model. All machines ran updated 42mm Öhlins forks and Polen generally used US-made C-CAT carbon brake discs while Falappa ran Brembo. After four years the weight was right on the minimum 140kg (309lb), with 52/48 per cent front to rear weight distribution. By taking advantage of the regulations the 1992 racers represented the quintessence of the 888.

After the striking dominance of 1991 Polen had a surprisingly slow start to the season. The team was in disarray and the testing of new components was done on the track in the early races. Roche led the way with

By 1992 the 888 was in its lightest and most potent incarnation. The frame was still the 1991 type, and there was extensive use of carbon fibre. *(Author's Collection)*

Riding for the official factory team, Polen had to work harder for the 1992 World Superbike Championship. *(Author's Collection)*

early victories at Albacete and Donington. Reverting to the 1991 set-up saw Polen take a double win at Hockenheim, and he eventually won nine races on the Dunlop-shod 888 to take his second title. Falappa was also on Dunlop this year, winning four races, and Roche remained with Michelin to take six victories. Polen also contested several AMA events on the Ferracci 888, but a conflict with World Superbike saw him take part in only seven races. He won three, and very nearly the Daytona 200, losing to Scott Russell by a mere 0.182 seconds. He still finished third in the championship.

There was again a catalogued 888 Racing available for 1992 although fewer were available. Thirty were produced during 1992, another during 1993, and a few 1992 specification machines up until 1995. For the first time the 888 Racing was genuinely competitive and Carl Fogarty rode one to a World Superbike victory at Donington in 1992. Edwin Weibel also won the German Pro-Superbike Championship. Like the factory racers, the 1992 888 Corsa was based on the 1991 production machines, with the earlier frame and styling. The 128bhp engine was similar to the 1991 888 Racing, but for a new exhaust camshaft and Termignoni exhaust system to widen the powerband. Like the factory racer more attention was paid to weight saving. There was a carbon fibre and Kevlar fuel tank with a quick release and safety valve, and a host of carbon fibre components like footpeg brackets. The weight was 150kg (331lb), still some way from the class minimum.

1993

Carl Fogarty's performances during 1992 earned him a factory ride alongside Falappa, and with Roche as team manager Rolando Simonetti joined as chief mechanic. Factory support also went to Team Grottini. Managed by Davide Tardozzi, the Grottini machines were tuned by Pietro di Gianesin for Juan Garriga and Stéphane Mertens. Mauro Lucchiari started the season on an 888 Corsa, but excellent results saw him also receive factory support.

Now close to the end of its life as an 888, the engine was initially similar to the 1992 version. However, the speed of Scott Russell's Kawasaki prompted a 96 x 64mm (926cc) engine for faster circuits. With 37 and 31mm valves, and an 11.9:1 compression ratio, the power was up to around 144bhp at 11,500rpm with Avgas 100. Nicknamed 'Il Pompone', or Big Pump, the 926 wasn't as responsive as the 138bhp 888, so the smaller engine continued to be used on tighter circuits. There was also was excessive blow-by from the Omega pistons that required a second crankcase breather. There was a Sprague-type anti-lock clutch to counteract rear wheel chatter, and considerable internal engine lightening to improve engine pick-up. This included titanium Pankl con-rods. There was a new stainless steel spaghetti-shaped exhaust system and the airbox was a one-piece sealed unit instead of the three-piece design of 1992. Double mapping now featured exclusively, as did variable length intakes. Simonetti also developed an electronic quick shifter and experimented with an early form of EPROM monitoring through a series of display modules on the dashboard.

The factory racers looked quite different for 1993 as they now featured the revised frame and Pierre Terblanche-designed 888 bodywork. This was homologated in July 1992, and provided slightly improved aerodynamics, even though the frame modifications were cosmetic. An increased ride height steepened the effective steering head angle and there was a new swingarm to accommodate a wider, 6.25-inch rear wheel. As the weight limit for twins was now 145kg (320lb), some components were stronger and heavier (noticeably the lower triple clamp). The 42mm Öhlins forks and shock absorber were also improved, and the front brakes generally 290mm carbon Brembo. 320mm steel discs were still used in wet conditions, and sometimes a cocktail of both types.

Falappa stunned everyone with three victories at the start of the season, but he then faded as the year turned into a battle between Fogarty and Russell. Although Fogarty won 11 races, inconsistency lost him the title. With development of the 916 also keeping the factory busy it appeared that their resources were stretched to the limit. Despite this, the 926 managed to win 19 races and the constructors' championship.

The 46 888 Racing machines built for 1993 shared the newly homologated frame and bodywork with the factory bikes, and with even more carbon fibre the weight was down to 145kg (320lb). Still 888cc, there were 36mm and 31mm valves, a new exhaust camshaft

There was new bodywork for the 926 racer of 1993, but after a year-long battle with Scott Russell, Fogarty had to settle for second. (Author's Collection)

(with 10.5mm of valve lift), and a larger airbox. This used the frame tubes to optimise the intake shape. The 400gm pistons were Mondial, there were chrome-molybdenum Pankl con-rods, and a revised combustion chamber design for the lower octane fuel. The power was 135bhp at 11,500rpm at the rear wheel. Other developments included a closer ratio six-speed gearbox, with the first four gears raised considerably, an improved clutch, and differential mapping for the two cylinders. The Brembo brakes and Marchesini three-spoke wheels were much as before, but there was evolutionary Öhlins suspension. Andreas Meklau rode a private 926cc machine to victory at Zeltweg, beating all the works machines. Doug Polen decided to attempt the AMA Superbike National Championship during 1993, winning six of the ten rounds. As the weight for twins was still 140kg (309lb), the Fast by Ferracci machine was a 1992 specification 888, now producing 142bhp. Polen and the FBF 888 were easily the strongest combination and Polen gave Ducati their first AMA Superbike Championship. Weibel repeated his win in the German Pro-Superbike Championship.

1994

As the racing department was limited in the number of new 916s it could produce, the customer 888 Racing for 1994 was much the same as the 1993 926cc factory racer. Thirty-two were built and they displaced 926cc. There were 37 and 31mm nimonic valves, 96mm 12:1 Omega pistons, titanium con-rods saving 160gm (5.6oz), and an improved crankcase design with a new crankcase breather and tank. There was also a new gear selector mechanism and an oil bleed. The crankshaft was also 800gm (28oz) lighter, and with a 48mm exhaust the power was 142 horsepower at 11,500rpm. There was a new airbox and the CPU was an IAW 435 (P8). The new frame with bent top tubes had a reduced steering head angle of 22°, and there were revised 42mm Öhlins front forks, shock absorber, and steering damper. The wheels were now five-spoke Marchesini, 3.50 x 17 and 6.00 x 17-inch. There was a mercury switch in case of a fall, new narrow-faced front disc rotors, a thinner rear disc, a revised rear brake anti-hop device, and new Michelin racing tyres. While the 888 was effectively

NEW GENERATION **129**

The 1994 Ferracci 955 represented the ultimate development of the 851 series, and despite the advent of the 916 was still a formidable racing machine.
(Author's Collection)

As a rookie from Down Under, Troy Corser gave Ducati a second AMA Superbike Championship in 1994.
(Steve Reeves)

superseded by the new 916, there were many initial problems setting the 916 up for racing. The tried and tested 888/926 was still an impressive performer in Superbike racing, particularly in the US and Germany.

For 1994 Australian Superbike Champion Troy Corser took Polen's place in the Ferracci team. Although the AMA racer was based on a 926 Corsa, Eraldo Ferracci installed a longer (66mm) stroke crankshaft from a 916. This gave a displacement of 955cc, and with around 155bhp made even more power than the factory 916 955cc racers because of a freer flowing exhaust allowed by the 888 chassis. It was also advantageous for Ferracci to run the older chassis during 1994 as this was very well developed and they could use the 1993 chassis set-up. For 1994 the weight for twins was increased to 152kg (335lb), but there was considerable controversy over the eligibility of Ferracci's 955. However, Ferracci had the factory develop a special 955 kit that included new cylinders, crankshaft, con-rods, and pistons. After three straight victories, the weight for twins was increased immediately to that of the fours, 162kg (358lb). Despite this handicap, Corser still narrowly won the championship. Udo Mark, meanwhile, continued the 888's reign in the German series.

THE SUPERMONO

As the story of racing Ducatis began with the single cylinder, and eventually begat the twin, it was logical that the Desmoquattro twin would in turn lead to the creation of a single. With the Supermono history turned full circle, but it was now from the perception of Massimo Bordi rather than Fabio Taglioni. During 1990 Bordi mapped out his plan, electing to adapt the current 90° V-twin so that vibration could be eliminated. His original idea called for a V-twin with a dummy piston, but internal friction and excessive crankcase pressure resulted in the 487cc (95.6 x 68mm) engine producing only 53bhp on its first dyno run. Even an increase to 57bhp proved disappointing, so Bordi incorporated a unique counterbalancing system with the second con-rod attached to a lever pivoting on a pin fixed in the crankcase. Titled the *doppia bielletta* (double con-rod), this was the first time it had been used on a petrol engine, although it had previously featured on diesel engines. Bordi was familiar with small direct injection diesels as these were what he initially worked on when he joined Ducati. The revised Supermono engine was not only more compact, but the twin's perfect primary balance was preserved without the burden of friction. Immediately the power went up to 62.5bhp at 10,500rpm. The next development saw a 502cc version (95.6 x 70mm) that produced 70bhp before the development team led by Gianluigi Mengoli and Claudio Domenicali created a larger cylinder with a wider stud pattern to allow for a 'closed deck' Nikasil 100mm cylinder and a British Omega 11.8:1 piston. This 549cc example produced 75bhp at 10,000rpm and was the version that went into limited production as a catalogue racer during 1993.

Many of the features of the Supermono were inherited from the 888 Racing. Along with liquid-cooling, and the double overhead camshaft four valve desmodromic cylinder head, it used an identical Weber IAW Alfa/N fuel injection system, with twin injectors and a 435 (P8) CPU. The throttle body diameter was 50mm tapering to 47mm at the butterfly, the valve sizes 37 and 31mm, and the camshafts had the same profile as the 926cc 1994 888 Racing. The camshafts, though, were 10mm (0.39in) shorter, with the exhaust having a slot machined to provide a takeoff for the water pump impeller. There were some important departures in the

When the 502cc Supermono was tested at Misano during 1992 it had bodywork derived from Pierre Terblanche's 888. There was also an aluminium rear subframe.
(Australian Motorcycle News)

Terblanche's definitive Supermono wasn't derivative, and the unique styling has been universally acclaimed. (Ian Falloon)

design, notably the use of much stronger 49mm plain main bearings and a dry, 180-watt alternator on the left with the water pump driven off the exhaust camshaft. Thus many engine components were specific to the Supermono, including the crankcases, cylinders, crankshaft, and gearbox with different ratios. As with the 888 Racing the two con-rods were titanium Pankl, with a length of 124mm (4.9in), a 21mm wristpin, and a 42mm big-end. Because of the plain main bearings oil pump flow was increased, to 3.3 litres per minute every 1,000rpm. The 50mm exhaust exited on the right, into either a Termignoni single or dual outlet muffler.

Housing this remarkable engine was a tubular steel frame built by Cagiva Telai in Varese, with an aluminium Verlicchi-made swingarm. Designed by Domenicali and Franco Bilancione at Varese, the frame was constructed from ALS 500 that provided the same stiffness-to-weight at a lower cost. With 22mm diameter tubing, with a 1.5mm wall thickness, the 6kg (13.2lb) design was TIG-welded. The rear suspension was by cantilever, but with a nine per cent rising rate due to the mounting angle. Only the highest quality suspension components were used, with 42mm Öhlins upside-down forks with magnesium triple clamps similar to those on the 888 Corsa. The Öhlins DU2041 shock absorber was adjustable for ride height via an eccentric.

Responsive handling was assured with a steering head angle of 23°, giving 92mm (3.6in) of trail, and the wheelbase was a compact 1,360mm (4ft 5.5in). This was 20mm (0.8in) less than Bordi originally anticipated, but even more significant was the weight distribution that placed 54.5 per cent on the front wheel. Marchesini three-spoke magnesium wheels in sizes of 3.50 x 17 and 5.00 x 17-inches were fitted, along with Brembo 280mm fully floating iron front discs, and racing P4.30–34 calipers. At the rear was a 190mm Brembo disc and P32A caliper. In order to keep the weight down to 122kg (269lb) every body part was of carbon fibre.

In mid 1992 Davide Tardozzi and Giancarlo Falappa tested the 502cc prototype at Misano. This had bodywork similar to Pierre Terblanche's 1992 888 update, but when the 549cc Supermono was finally displayed at the Cologne Show in September it had new bodywork, also by Terblanche. Only receiving a bare chassis in July, Terblanche worked at Cagiva Morrazone in Varese, creating the bodywork in two months. From the outset,

The Supermono was also an extremely effective racing motorcycle for its genre. Robert Holden raced one to victory in the 1995 Singles TT at the Isle of Man. (Ian Falloon)

Bordi had considerable difficulty in convincing the marketing department of the viability of the Supermono as a production motorcycle. Eventually it was launched only as a catalogue racer for Sounds of Singles racing. Thirty were manufactured in 1993, plus a further ten in 1994.

Mauro Lucchiari campaigned a factory racing Supermono during 1993 (with a heavily braced swingarm and larger 300mm front discs), and at the Isle of Man Robert Holden finished second in the 1994 Single Cylinder TT. He came back in 1995 to win easily, setting a fastest lap of 111.66mph (179.66kmh). Even when it was released the Supermono was too small to challenge the specialised single cylinder competition and for 1995 there was a larger 572cc version. Apart from the 102mm piston there were few changes. There was also a revised EPROM and silencer, slightly revised 42mm Öhlins FG9311 front forks with magnesium triple clamps, and a 10mm (0.39in) longer DU2042 rear shock absorber. Twenty-five of the 572cc series were constructed but they were still outclassed in ultimate power output. In the European SuperMono Cup, a support event to World Superbike, the Ducati Supermono won only once, at Donington in 1998 in the hands of Callum Ramsay. Racing journalist Alan Cathcart came close to winning the series in 1996, and at Daytona in 1998 Jon Cornwell won the AHRMA Supermono race.

Probably the most important function of the Supermono was its use as a test bed for the World Superbike racers. In 1991 95.6mm pistons were tried on the racers and during 1993 much was learnt about high piston speeds with a 70mm stroke and a 100mm piston. Lucchiari's racer was consistently revved to 11,500rpm and this experience paid dividends when the twins finally featured 100mm pistons. Work with the pressurised airbox also led to the 916's improved airbox design. Ultimately the Supermono was left with nowhere to go. Even when it was conceived its capacity was too small, and the design was limited to 600cc with the existing components. As Singles racing gradually died there was even less demand for the Supermono. And in a racing world that requires continual development the Supermono still lay somewhere back in 1992. It may have been a beautiful and, within its parameters, effective creation, but in Ducati racing terms the Supermono is an anomaly – a machine without a purpose, and one without any real race success to its name.

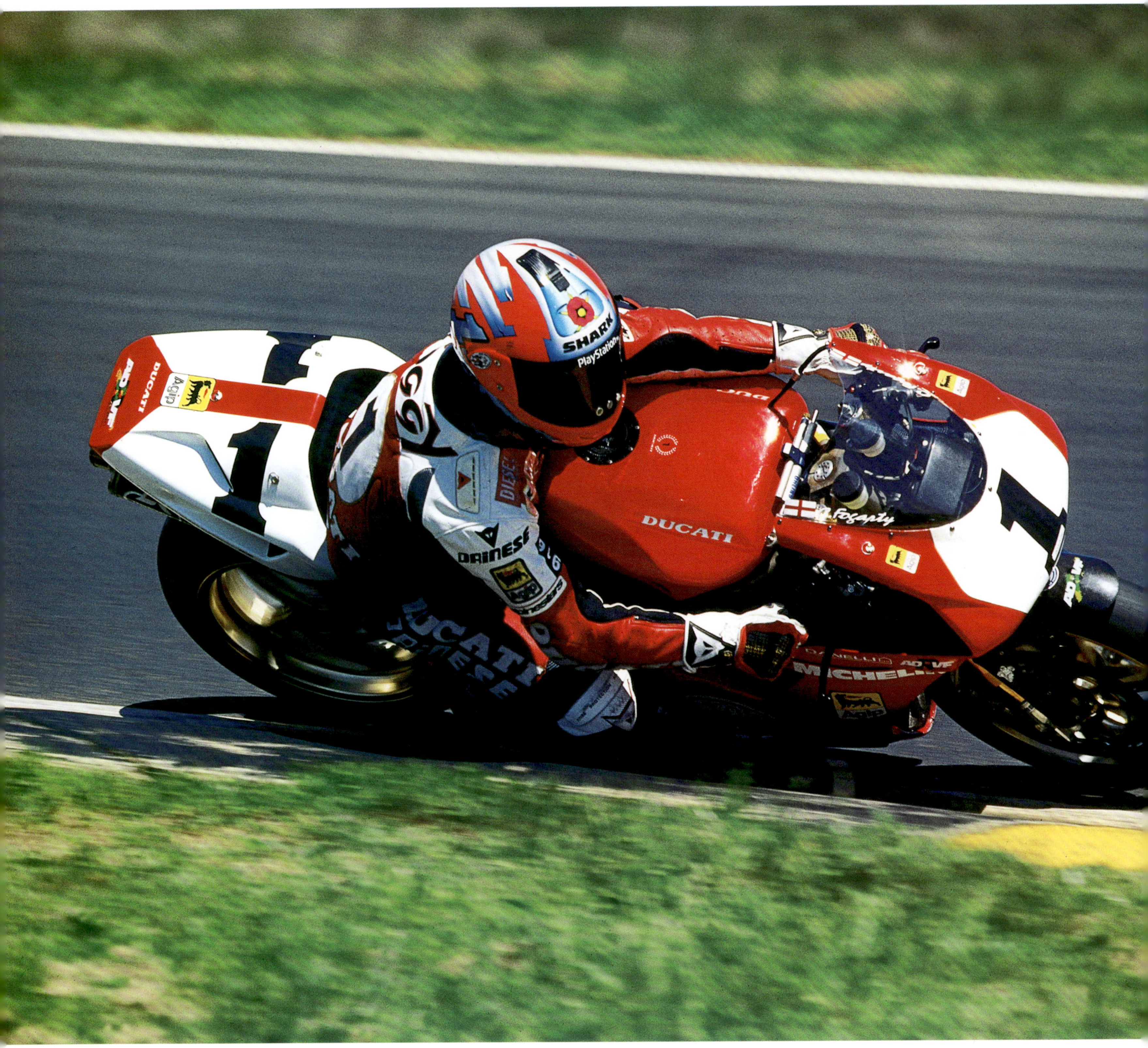
SHARK
PlayStation
DUCATI
DAINESE
MICHELIN
Fogarty

8 THE 916 AND BEYOND

Fogarty totally dominated the 1995 season, but switched to Honda in 1996. (Ian Falloon)

The release of the 916 at the end of 1993 changed Ducati forever. Before the 916, Ducati was associated with individual and slightly eccentric desmodromic motorcycles for the cognoscenti. After the 916 Ducati was accepted as a mainstream motorcycle, and desmodromics lost much of their mystery. This was reflected in the production numbers. 851 and 888 production between 1987 and 1994 totalled 10,315. Over a similar period (1993–2000), production of the 748/916/996/998 was more than five times that of the earlier Desmoquattro, at 53,456. Ducati history changed forever with the birth of the 916.

Much of the mystique of the 916 and its descendants was associated with its racing success. Although it continued a racing tradition that began back in 1955 with the Marianna, unlike earlier designs that faded after a few years its dominance has continued. There was so much room left for development that, even as the design approaches its tenth anniversary, it maintains its position as the quintessential World Superbike racer.

Before the advent of the World Superbike Championship the Castiglioni brothers had plans for a Desmoquattro designed from the ground up specifically for racing. While Massimo Bordi and his team at Bologna were steadily developing the 888, Massimo Tamburini at Rimini was at work creating a new Desmoquattro, the 916. The 916 marked a huge change in direction for the company. Rather than a production of continual evolution, Tamburini set about designing the motorcycle as an entity. He embarked upon the project during 1987, and so concentrated was the development that it lasted six years. During that time the project expanded to include 25 engineers. The preliminary mock-up first appeared during 1991, and by January 1992 the frame configuration was complete. Built by Cagiva Telai, the diameter of the main frame tubing (25 CrMo4) was 28mm, with the secondary tubing the same as that on the 888 at 22mm. There was also an additional lower engine support, contributing to increased rigidity and providing additional swingarm support. An important component of the structure was the racer's sealed carbon fibre airbox, increasing frame rigidity by 20 per cent, and to improve the weight distribution the engine was rotated forward 1° for the front tyre to clear the cylinder head.

One of the significant features of the new frame was its exceptionally strong steering head structure, with 80mm diameter tubing and offering adjustable caster (to 23° for racing) through ellipsoidal bearings in the steering tube. Another impressive feature was the design of the triple clamps, machined in pairs, with a deep chill-cast lower triple clamp. As Bordi was still interested in pursuing success in endurance racing, there was a single-sided swingarm to enable rapid wheel changes. The exhaust system curving up under the seat was also designed to aid aerodynamics more than ultimate power. Another requirement was a reduction in frontal area and an improvement in aerodynamics over the 888, so the final design was extremely compact.

While Tamburini was working on the chassis, Massimo Bordi was busy at Bologna developing the Desmoquattro engine. The goal was always to eventually produce a full litre engine so Bordi lengthened the 888 stroke 2mm, to 66mm. Although the street bike displaced 916cc with 94mm pistons, the factory racer was immediately bored to 955cc. The crankshaft was similar to the 888, with titanium Pankl 124mm (4.9in) con-rods with a 21mm gudgeon (up from 20mm on the street bike), and a 45mm big-end journal. The longer stroke also provided more headroom in the combustion chamber and improved torque.

After losing the riders' championship during 1993, Ducati took a qualified gamble on immediately racing the unproven 916. Davide Tardozzi had undertaken much of the frame and suspension testing at Mugello, so the Castiglionis were confident the new machine was race ready. They were right, and the 916 was immediately competitive.

1994

For the 1994 season Virginio Ferrari replaced Roche as manager of the official racing team. Ferrari was also a leading rider, having won the 1985 Italian F1 Championship on a TT1. His rider line-up of Carl Fogarty and Giancarlo Falappa was unchanged, but this would be Falappa's final season. Another serious crash, whilst testing at Albacete in June, ended his racing career.

Developments to the 916 engine included 96mm forged Omega 11.6:1 pistons, and 37mm inlet and 31mm exhaust valves. Experimentation with titanium valves resulted in several engine failures throughout the season. New moderate lift (11mm inlet and 10.5mm exhaust) long duration camshafts, with extremely steep opening and closing ramps, also caused valve rocker failure. The Marelli P8 CPU was mounted in the fairing in front of the steering head, with separate mapping for each cylinder. There were 50mm throttle bodies (46mm at the butterfly), and with 4.5 Bar fuel pressure and 102 octane AVGAS the 955 produced 150bhp at 11,000rpm at the gearbox.

This year the weight of the 750cc fours was reduced to 160kg (353lb), while the twins remained at 145kg (320lb). To get close to this minimum there were magnesium engine covers, and all the bodywork was in carbon fibre, with the fairing reinforced by Kevlar. A further 3kg (6.6lb) was saved with a digital instrument panel. The suspension was Öhlins, with 46mm forks, but there were initial handling problems. To improve traction, and place more weight on the front wheel, Tamburini designed a 20mm (0.8in) longer magnesium swingarm. This saved 1kg (2.2lb), pushing the weight bias forward, and featured a 50mm (up from 35mm) axle. The wheelbase was increased 8mm to 1,428mm (4ft 8.2in), and the ride height raised through a new rear suspension lever. The front brakes were twin Brembo 320mm cast-iron, or 290mm carbon. There was a

Even though it was a new design, Carl Fogarty found the 916 good enough to give it a debut victory at Donington. *(Ian Falloon)*

By the end of the 1994 season the 916 factory racer was much improved and Fogarty sealed the championship at Phillip Island. This was the final year for carbon brakes in World Superbike. *(Ian Falloon)*

Right: Nothing distinguished Fogarty more than his penetrating eyes. *(Ian Falloon)*

Opposite top: In his final racing season, Giancarlo Falappa won one World Superbike race on the 916. This is at Donington on the first 916 with the shorter swingarm, Falappa leading 1993 champion Scott Russell. *(Ian Falloon)*

Opposite bottom: For 1995 the 955cc racer had steel brake discs, new Öhlins suspension, and the longer magnesium swingarm. *(Ian Falloon)*

CARL FOGARTY

As Ducati's most successful World Superbike racer, 'King' Carl Fogarty (or Foggy) has done more to promote the company's racing image than anyone. The success of both the 916 and the World Superbike Championship is largely a result of Fogarty's racing achievements. With four World Superbike championships and 59 race wins (55 on Ducati), Fogarty has a record that looks unlikely to be bettered.

Born in Blackburn, Lancashire, on 1 July 1965, Carl Fogarty followed in his father George's footsteps. George was a successful racer in his own right, riding Ducatis for Sports Motorcycles while Carl was a teenager. This family association led to Carl winning his first World Superbike race at Donington in 1992 on a Sports Motorcycles 888 Corsa. Earlier Carl proved himself on the most demanding and dangerous circuit, the Isle of Man. In 1988 he rode a Honda RC30 to victory in the F1 TT, and won the TTF1 World Championship. He repeated this in 1989 and 1990.

In 1992 Fogarty struggled to find a fully sponsored ride so accepted an offer to ride for the French Kawasaki endurance team. Against the odds, Fogarty and Terry Rymer beat all the fancied endurance specialists and won the World Endurance Championship. The Superbike win at Donington saw him as a wildcard entry in the British Grand Prix on a Cagiva 500, where he proved one of the few modern riders that could successfully race on a closed-road or purpose built racetrack. In 1992 Fogarty also set an Isle of Man lap record that would last seven years.

After winning two World Superbike Championships with Ducati, Fogarty surprised everyone, including Virginio Ferrari, by changing camps for Honda at the end of 1995. He took with him his mechanic, Tony 'Slick' Bass, but struggled to come to terms with the Honda RC45. It wasn't until Assen, where he scored a memorable double victory, that Fogarty proved to his detractors that he couldn't only ride a Ducati. After that one hiccup, Fogarty remained with Ducati, and looked ominously dominant by the end of 1999. That was when his career went awry. A pre-2000 season testing accident and a serious crash in the second round at Australia ended his career. After a test at Mugello in September he confirmed his retirement, but his legacy remains. In England Fogarty became the first motorcycle racing superstar since Barry Sheene. He gave motorcycle racing prominence and gained such a following that huge crowds went to World Superbike races. More recently he may have turned his back on the company that gave him everything, but Fogarty and Ducati will forever remain synonymous.

200mm carbon disc on the rear and wheels were three-spoke, and later five-spoke, Marchesini 3.50 and 6.00 x 17-inch.

The racing department produced 14 916 Racing machines during 1994, and they were only provided to selected teams. Fabrizio Pirovano (riding for Davide Tardozzi) and James Whitham (for Moto Cinelli) supported the factory team in World Superbike, with four rides by Troy Corser on a Fast by Ferracci entry. Fogarty gave the 916 a victory at Donington, continuing the tradition of debut victories. After he broke his wrist at Hockenheim in May Russell broke away but Fogarty fought back to take the championship in the final race of the season. Along the way Fogarty won ten races, and with Falappa and Whitham also taking victories the Ducati 916 won the constructors' title in its first season.

1995

Mauro Lucchiari joined Fogarty in Ferrari's ADVF team, with official factory machines also supplied to Troy Corser riding for Alfred Inzinger's Promotor team (managed by Tardozzi). Each rider received two bikes, but no one was prepared for the improvement that the racing department had managed to obtain from the 955 during the winter. Engine development concentrated on improving reliability rather than outright power and there were stronger crankcases, now without the kick-start boss, and new nimonic valves (still 37 and 31mm). The engine still displaced 955cc (with 11.8:1 Omega pistons) but in the first and final races Fogarty tried a 996cc engine (with 98mm pistons). He found that the extra mid-range power detrimentally affected the handling so preferred the 955. There was a slipper clutch and 52mm exhausts, no longer featuring a crossover tube joining the two headers. Running on unleaded fuel, the power was 154bhp at 12,000rpm at the crankshaft.

New regulations banned carbon brake discs, and there were twin Brembo steel 320mm front discs and a 220mm rear. The brake calipers were Brembo P4.32/36 and P2.24, and the 46mm Öhlins forks and Öhlins shock absorber were updated. The wheels were five-spoke Marchesini, a 3.50 and 6.25 x 17-inch. With the initial minimum weight increased to only 147kg (324lb) for twins Fogarty and Lucchiari raced away from the rest of the field in the opening rounds. This success saw a revision of the minimum weights and from Monza the twins were required to weigh 155kg (342lb), with the 750 fours reduced to 160kg (353lb). To increase the weight a non-functioning starter motor was installed, and lead ballast added under the seat. As Virginio Ferrari told the author, 'much of our advantage was due to the use of electronic telemetry during qualifying, and recruiting Anders Andersson as a full time Öhlins suspension technician.' The 1995 955 factory racer provided an optimum balance that was difficult to replicate. Fogarty won 13 races, and had the championship sealed with two rounds to spare. The other Ducati riders also shared in the spoils. Corser won four races, Lucchiari two, and Chili one (on the Gattolone 916 Racing).

The 1995 customer 916 Racing was closely patterned on Fogarty's 1994 factory bike. Displacing 955cc, it had the same camshaft timing, valve sizes, and closer ratio gearbox. The Marelli injection system featured twin injectors and a P8 CPU. The compression ratio was 12:1 and the power was 155bhp at 11,500rpm. The chassis specification was also similar to the 1994 factory machine. There was a 10mm (0.39in) longer swingarm, giving a wheelbase of 1,420mm (4ft 7.9in), and a larger 22-litre (4.8gal) carbon fibre fuel tank. The suspension was Öhlins 46mm FG9650 forks, with an Öhlins DU5360 rear shock absorber, and brakes were racing Brembo twin 320mm cast-iron discs with P4.32–36mm calipers and a 19mm master cylinder on the front and a 200mm disc with a P2.24mm master cylinder and 11mm master cylinder on the rear. The wheels were five-spoke Marchesini 3.50 and 6.00 x 17-inches. Weighing 154kg (340lb), 60 916 Racing machines were available for teams throughout the world and they were very competitive. Chili rode Pietro di Gianesin's Team Gattolone machine to victory in a World Superbike race at Monza, Steve Hislop won the British Superbike Championship, and Matt Llewellyn the Shell Advance International Superbike Trophy. In the US Eraldo Ferracci recruited Freddie Spencer to ride the 916, who won at Laguna Seca in the rain, though his overall performance was disappointing.

During 1995 there was also a brief return to Endurance racing, with two 955 Endurance racers entered in the Bol d'Or in September. Andreas Meklau teamed with Mauro Lucchiari while Stéphane Chambon put the other 955 on pole position. Although the new reinforced crankcases survived 36 hours on the test bench and promised increased reliability, both the works machines retired.

1996

Despite Cagiva's financial crisis, there was an expanded racing programme for 1996. Ferrari signed former 250cc World Champion John Kocinski and Neil Hodgson, while Promotor retained Corser and signed Mike Hale. Kocinski, Hodgson, and Corser received full factory machinery, although Hale's was of a lesser specification. In addition to the six official machines, Pietro di Gianesin's Gattolone team also received factory support.

There were thicker crankcase castings for the 996cc engines and all the factory motors ran three-ring 98mm 12:1 Omega pistons. The 37 and 31mm valves were now a composite design (titanium with steel at the top of the stem to reduce wear), and there were new 32/59 (1.84:1) primary gears to spread the tooth load more evenly. The throttle bodies increased to 54mm (48mm at the butterfly), there were 54mm diameter exhausts, and larger water and oil radiators. Breathing was improved through a larger airbox (with larger ducts), created by moving the radiator header tank forward. The fuel pressure was increased to five Bar and the engine covers were aluminium rather than magnesium. The power was 157bhp at 11,800rpm at the gearbox, but there were many engine failures. Adapting the 916 engine cases for 98mm pistons resulted in smaller diameter cylinder studs (6mm), and the restricted stud spacing allowed for only a 3mm thick liner. Most engine failures were the result of the cylinder liner breaking where it entered the crankcase, although there were also oil pressure problems caused by wheelies.

The weight of the twins was now the same as that of the fours, at 162kg (357lb), so the emphasis was on increasing the front end bias. Braking was now marginal so there were new 46mm Öhlins forks with adjustable offset triple clamps that spread the discs 28mm (1.1in) further apart for improved cooling. The front Brembo calipers were P4.34/36mm and there was a new Öhlins rear suspension unit. The wheels were five-spoke magnesium Marchesini, a 3.50 and a 6.00 x 17-inch. Permanently installed, and adding 4kg (8.8lb), was the PI System 3 Plus data acquisition system.

Although Kocinski won five races, his relationship with Ferrari deteriorated to such an extent that by midway through the season there was no communication between them, destroying team morale. This allowed Corser to win seven races, and the championship.

There was a further batch of 31 955 Racing machines for 1996. Visually identical to the 1995 version apart from the absence of air vents in the tail, there were a number of changes. Still 955cc, engine developments included new crankcases, aluminium side covers, new 96mm pistons, and new con-rod bearings. There was also an inlet camshaft patterned on the 1995 factory racer. The exhaust system was enlarged to 52mm, there was a clutch with a back torque limiter, a steel gearshift selector drum, new timing belts and an oil pump with an enclosed relief valve. With a slightly lower 11.8:1 compression ratio, the power was 153bhp at 11,000rpm. Chassis developments included new 46mm Öhlins forks (now with a top-out spring), thicker front brake discs (6mm), and an aluminium casing and fast preload adjuster for the Öhlins DU5360 rear shock absorber. The fuel capacity was up to 23 litres (5.1gal), and the weight 160kg (353lb).

The 955 Racing was also very successful. On the Gattolone machine Pier Francesco Chili won two World Superbike races, while Paolo Casoli won the Italian Superbike Championship. Christer Lindholm won the German Pro-Superbike Championship, and Andreas Meklau the Austrian Superbike Championship. Results weren't quite as good in the US. Larry Pegram and Shawn Higbee's poor results prompted Ducati to enter 1992 125cc World Champion Alessandro Gramigni in four races. Gramigni immediately impressed, winning at Elkhart Lake and Brainerd, but it wasn't enough to win the championship. In the British Superbike Championship Terry Rymer won five rounds on the Old Spice 955, but could only manage third overall.

The factory racers displaced 996cc for 1996, and with the minimum weight increasing to 162kg (357lb) there were aluminium engine covers. (Author's Collection)

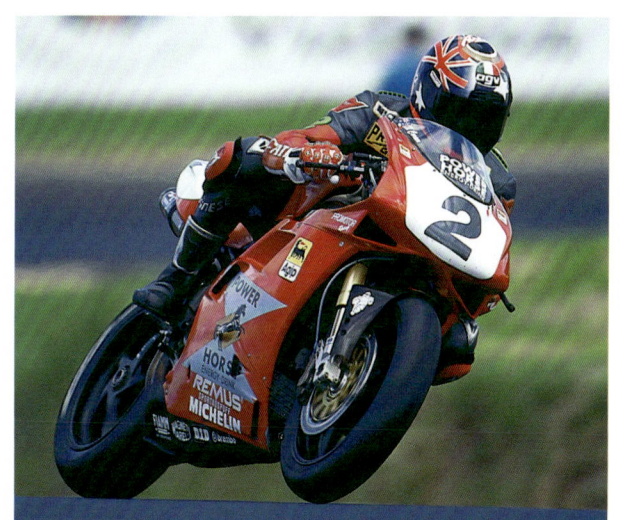

After a season where no single rider dominated, Troy Corser eventually took the 1996 title on the Promotor 996. (Ian Falloon)

Much was expected of John Kocinski, but despite flashes of brilliance he disappointed. (Ian Falloon)

After returning to Ducati in 1998 Corser spent two years in the shadow of Fogarty and was unceremoniously sacked at the end of the 1999 season. *(Ian Falloon)*

TROY CORSER

Attempting to emulate his countrymen Wayne Gardner and Mick Doohan, Troy Corser's first road race was in 1989 on a Honda CR125. Corser was born on 27 November 1971 in Woollongong, New South Wales, Australia, and he began competing in local enduro races at the age of ten. After switching to road racing, his rise in Australia was meteoric, culminating in his winning the 1993 Australian Superbike Championship on the theoretically obsolete Honda RC30. This led Corser to the AMA Superbike Championship (he was the first non-American to win the title). Fogarty's switch to Honda gave Corser the break he needed and he smoothly carved his way to victory in the 1996 World Superbike Championship. From there on his career was punctuated by misfortune and mistakes.

Electing to stay with Promotor during 1997, Corser made a move into 500cc Grands Prix on a YZR Yamaha. This was an unmitigated disaster. Inzinger's empire collapsed and Corser only competed in seven races. He was back with Ferrari's Ducati team for 1998 but blew the championship with a crash on the warm-up lap at the final round in Sugo. Throughout 1999 he rode under the shadow of Fogarty, and after finishing third in the championship was unceremoniously sacked by Ducati late in the season. With nowhere left to go but to the struggling Aprilia, Corser then showed his ability by winning five races in 2000 – this on a machine that had previously barely finished in the points. Although criticised for his inconsistency, when it comes to the single lap SuperPole Corser is the undisputed master.

1997

Following the Texas Pacific Group buy-in of Ducati towards the end of 1996 there was an immediate expansion of the World Superbike racing programme for 1997. Virginio Ferrari's team of Fogarty and Hodgson received full works support, as did Andrea Merloni's Gattolone Team of Pier Francesco Chili.

There were eight factory machines, and with the homologation of new crankcases with a wider stud pattern, via the 916 SPS, there were now thicker cylinder liners for the 98mm pistons. As the crankcases were heavier, less ballast was required. There was also experimentation with a bolt-on sump extension to alleviate the oil pressure drop under acceleration and braking. The new cylinder heads had larger inlet ports and a revised combustion chamber. There was also a new gearbox and exhaust system, larger capacity oil and water radiators, and an increase in the throttle body diameter to 60mm (2.36in). Regulations now required a reduction in exhaust levels to 102db/A (from 105db/A), but the power was around 168bhp at 11,300rpm at the gearbox.

Chassis developments included a 1.5kg (3.3lb) heavier frame, with a 2kg (4.4lb) lighter cast magnesium swingarm to improve the front weight bias. The 46mm Öhlins forks had magnesium sliders and a new top out spring, with the travel increased 5mm to 125mm (4.9in). The 320mm stainless steel brake discs were 1mm thicker and spaced more widely apart for additional cooling, while the Brembo front brake calipers had larger pistons. Other chassis modifications included a reduction in rear rim width, to 5.75 x 17-inch, and a reshaping of the carbon fibre and Kevlar fuel tank with an increase in capacity to 24 litres (5.3gal).

Although the engine developments aided reliability, in all other respects the 996 was inferior. There were too many changes from the successful 955 and the supreme balance of that machine was lost. The 60mm throttle bodies and lighter crankshaft provided an aggressive power delivery that upset the handling, and the weight distribution was unsatisfactory. Throughout the season there was experimentation with an even longer swingarm, smaller (290mm) front brake discs to quicken the steering response, and higher profile Michelin

Development for 1997 followed the wrong path, and the 996cc factory racer was extremely difficult to ride. *(Author's Collection)*

Despite the difficulties he experienced with the machine, Fogarty still managed second in the championship. *(Phil Aynsley)*

rear tyres. Fogarty remained openly unhappy with the performance of the 996, but still managed second place in the World Superbike Championship with six victories, while Chili also complained about the power delivery but won three races. But for the first time since 1990 Ducati failed to win the World Superbike constructors' championship.

The 20 1997 specification 996 Racing machines also featured the newly homologated crankcases, with 98mm 12:1 pistons. There was a new exhaust camshaft, new valve rocker arms, and the 32/59 tooth primary drive. The fuel pressure was increased to 5 Bar and there was a larger capacity airbox, a larger oil radiator, and 54mm exhaust headers. The power was 155bhp at 11,000rpm. Chassis developments included adjustable offset triple clamps, a larger air intake in the front fairing, new handlebars, and a revised rear hub assembly. On the 996 Racing Serafino Foti won the Italian Superbike Championship, and Andreas Meklau again took out the Austrian Superbike Championship. In the US factory support went to Ferracci and Vance & Hines. Ferracci signed Matthew Mladin while Vance & Hines hired former champion Thomas Stevens. They also recruited Christer Lindholm for the final race. The Ducati line-up looked strong, and while Mladin won four AMA Superbike races inconsistency robbed him of the title. Ducati also struggled in the UK. Although the Reve Red Bull team of John Reynolds and Steve Hislop, and the GSE (Groundwork South East) team of Sean Emmett, looked impressive, the Ducatis only managed three race wins.

1998

A further expansion of the racing programme for the 1998 World Superbike Championship saw 18 factory 996 racers built, again with three riders supported in two official teams. Troy Corser returned to the Ferrari Team alongside Chili, and Fogarty moved to the new Team Ducati Performance, managed by Davide Tardozzi. To address the problem of power delivery there was a new electronic injection system. Derived from Ferrari Formula One racing, the Magneti Marelli MF3-S system incorporated a third injector located outboard from each velocity-stack and inside the sealed airbox. Only operating at 70 per cent to full throttle when the primary injectors were shut off, as these third injectors were positioned further from the inlet valve they helped cooler, and denser, air enter the combustion chamber. Another advantage of the new system was the ability to download data through a laptop computer connected to the onboard computer via a Marelli DAS3 data acquisition system. There were also redesigned air intakes and airbox, and a new Termignoni exhaust system with reverse cones incorporated in the mufflers. Also incorporated in the crankcase was the sump extension with a lower oil pickup first tried during 1997. Retaining the 60mm throttle bodies, the power was around 163bhp at 12,000rpm at the rear wheel.

The engine was located slightly more forward in the 25CrMo4 frame. To placate suspension problems this was not as stiff as before and there was experimentation with swingarms. Öhlins finally supplied Grand Prix quality suspension, the 46mm forks having magnesium sliders and the triple clamps providing variable offset. At the rear a new Öhlins TT44 'double tube' rear suspension unit was sometimes used. The TT44 featured separate twin internal oil tubes for compression and rebound damping. The Brembo front brakes were either 320mm or 290mm steel discs, with a choice of two or four-pad front brake calipers. The quest for improved steering and traction also led to experimentation with different wheel sizes, including both 16 and 17-inch front Marchesinis, and either 16.5-inch or 17-inch rear wheels. The change in weight distribution saw 53/54 per cent on the front wheel, with 46/47 per cent on the rear wheel.

Early in the season the 996 lacked power but this improved following the South African round at Kyalami in early July. Here a new frame (homologated through the 916 SPS Fogarty Replica) allowed the rear bracing tube to be moved back and downwards. The engine was located slightly lower, and altering one of the top transverse frame tubes under the fuel tank provided room for a larger airbox, with the air intake, throttle bodies, and shorter intakes inside the airbox itself. New cylinder heads positioned the exhaust camshafts closer to the centre of the engine, providing more front wheel clearance, and there was a revised valve angle to improve fuel delivery. Along

Although it began the 1998 season underpowered, a new frame and airbox after Kyalami again saw the 996 back in contention for the championship. (Ian Falloon)

with new camshafts these developments provided a dramatic improvement. The torque curve became flatter, there was even more top-end power (reputedly 7–8bhp), and the handling improved. This small modification was undoubtedly the most effective single development to the 916 since its inception, and at the first race at Kyalami 996s filled the top three places. Fogarty narrowly won his third World Superbike title but only won three races during the season.

There were 24 996 Racing machines produced for 1998, with the specification following that of the 1997 factory machines. There was a new crankshaft and con-rod assembly, along with an improved primary drive and spline coupling. Small developments to aid reliability saw different crankshaft shimming, a new crankshaft inlet oil seal, and bigger rimmed timing belt rollers. The larger capacity water radiator was thicker, with three extra rows. There was a new gearshift drum, and the injection system included 60mm throttle bodies with new manifolds, still with the twin injector P8 CPU. The valve sizes remained at 37 and 31mm, and the claimed power was 151bhp at 11,000rpm.

New for the 996 Racing was a revised chassis, the TIG-welded 25CrMo4 frame using 1.5mm tubing, and a lighter rear subframe. A longer magnesium swingarm increased the wheelbase to 1,430mm (4ft 8.3in), also improving the weight distribution. The 46mm Öhlins fork was from the 1997 factory bike and the Öhlins rear shock absorber featured hydraulic adjustment for the spring preload. The front brakes were either 320mm or 290mm, and there was a larger, and reshaped, 24-litre (5.3gal) fuel tank. The claimed weight was 154kg (340lb), allowing fine tuning of the weight distribution through ballast. The 996 Racing won the Italian and German Superbike Championships. Paolo Blora won in Italy, and Andreas Meklau in Germany. Again there were two factory supported teams in the US. Mike Hale and Tom Kipp rode for Ferracci, with Anthony Gobert and Thomas Stevens for Vance & Hines. Gobert won three races, but it wasn't enough to win the championship. In the UK Emmett joined Reynolds in the Reve Red Bull Team, while Australian Troy Bayliss joined the GSE team. Despite this formidable line-up, this increasingly prestigious championship again eluded Ducati.

Casoli narrowly missing out on winning the 2000 World Supersport Championship on a Team Ducati Infostrada 748 R. *(Ian Falloon)*

RACING 748S:
THE 748 RACING AND RACING SPECIAL

Held as a support race to World Superbike, the 1995 European Supersport Championship was tailor made for the new 748 SP. Few modifications were allowed and Michael Paquay won seven races on the Team Alstare 748 SP, to win the championship. For the 1996 Open Supersport Championship Fabrizio Pirovano rode the Team Alstare 748 SP, winning five races and the championship. 1997 saw the establishment of the Supersport World Cup, and this time Paolo Casoli won the title on the Gio.Ca.Moto 748 SP. As Supersport racing gained in popularity 20 748 Racing machines were made available to selected teams for 1998. Assembled in the racing department, modifications were limited, but these were quite sophisticated machines. They retained the single injector IAW 1.6 M CPU, but featured a 916 Racing gearbox with a stronger clutch with sintered clutch plates. There were 33 and 29mm nimonic valves, and a 180-watt alternator. Homologated through the 748 SPS were shorter (33mm) carbon fibre inlet manifolds, incorporated as part of the throttle body after the throttle valve. There was also a 916 Racing cooling system, and a racing exhaust with carbon fibre mufflers. The power was 108bhp at 11,500rpm. Regulations allowed more latitude in the modification of the chassis, and there was complete carbon fibre bodywork, sump guard, chain guard and mufflers, front dashboard, and electronic control unit mount. With racing-only wiring and instrumentation, the weight was 170kg (375lb).

Paolo Casoli rode the factory 748 Racing in the 1998 Supersport World Series but his results were disappointing. Altered regulations tipped the balance towards the four-cylinder machines, and although he won two races Casoli could only manage fourth overall. His Ducati Performance 748 produced 117bhp at the rear wheel. For the 1999 season 18 similar 748 Racing machines were produced. The series became the World Supersport Championship and Ducati Performance again entered Paolo Casoli on their 748. This year the 748 was totally outclassed and with Casoli missing much of the season through injury he could only manage 14th in the championship.

As the 748 Racing was plainly outclassed, for the 2000 season Ducati Corse produced a considerably higher specification 748 RS (Racing Special). Based on the new production 748 R, this featured a newly homologated frame and airbox and an injection system similar to that of the 996 Factory racer. A single Marelli IWP 069 injector was placed above the throttle valve, with the throttle body inside the airbox and very short intake ducts. The injection system was the production IAW 1.6 M, but with 54mm throttle body. There were also a number of engine developments, including new camshafts, a 12:1 compression ratio, Menon chrome-topped racing 36mm and 30mm valves, a closer ratio gearbox, and a 0.78kg (1.72lb) lighter flywheel. There was a new water pump and larger radiator, wider (19mm) exposed cam belts and new pulleys. With 54mm racing titanium Termignoni exhaust system the power was an impressive 124bhp at 12,000rpm.

Regulations required that the chassis be production based, and apart from a new generation 'Mark II' Öhlins shock absorber with internal bleeds, and a one-piece rear wheel nut, it was the same as the 748 R. The racer had a different electrical system, with a tri-phase 280-watt alternator. Fifty-two 748 RSs were produced for 2000, of which Team Ducati Infostrada ran two, Paolo Casoli being joined by Ruben Xaus. Pietro di Gianesin prepared the engines, and the RS was immediately more competitive than the 748 R. Casoli won at Monza and at Brands Hatch, and Xaus at Assen, with Casoli finishing a close second in the championship.

Ducati Corse appeared to lose interest in pursuing the World Supersport Championship but a further batch of 42 748 RS was produced for 2001. Apart from the updated Öhlins forks and Brembo brakes of the production 748 R these were ostensibly the same as those of the previous year. The Dienza team of Vittoriano Guareschi and Dean Thomas had the best machines, but they were totally overrun by the Japanese four-cylinder 600s. Considering the 748 was always a 916 with a smaller engine it proved remarkably competitive over a long period, and was the only twin cylinder 750 to mount any challenge in this cut-throat class.

1999

A reorganisation of the racing programme for 1999 saw the establishment of Ducati Corse. Under the control of Claudio Domenicali, there was now only one World Superbike team, Tardozzi's Team Ducati Performance, with Fogarty and Corser the only riders. Filling out the grid were a number of assisted customer teams on 996 RSs. Continued engine development saw thicker cylinder head castings to increase rigidity, also allowing reshaped ports and re-angled valves. With the same triple injector MF3-S injection system with differential mapping between the cylinders, there was a revised airbox and intake tracts. A close ratio Evolution gearbox was also available and development centred on providing less power drop-off throughout the rev range. There was a 57mm stainless steel exhaust system and an improvement in reliability. The power was 168bhp at 11,500rpm at the rear wheel.

In an effort to improve front tyre feel and replicate the balance of the earlier 955, there were smaller diameter (42mm) Öhlins front forks. Although not as stiff they reduced unsprung weight and provided mounts for the new generation of Brembo radial four-piston brake calipers. The more rigid caliper location improved braking, and smaller (290mm) discs improved the steering response. There was also a new Öhlins TT44 shock absorber with all new hydraulics, and a revised rear suspension linkage with a constant rate (2:1) to reduce rear wheel chatter. To improve rider aerodynamics there was a smaller fuel tank, slimmer and 20mm (0.79in) lower, and extending more into the airbox.

These developments paid off and Fogarty dominated the World Superbike Championship almost in the manner of 1995. Fogarty won eleven races, Corser three, with Gobert and Ben Bostrom one apiece. Throughout the season the 996 also underwent continual evolution. As the official Ducati Corse testing and development rider, Paolo Casoli rode the 996 Factory Evolution racer to victory in every round of the Italian Superbike Championship. Continual improvements filtered through to the World Superbike racers. However, as they were performing well the single injector fuel injection system, with the throttle butterfly even closer to the valves, was held over for 2000.

Left: In the early days of European and World Supersport racing the 748 SP was dominant. Paolo Casoli won the 1997 championship on the Gio.Ca.Moto entry. *(Ian Falloon)*

Right: Improvements to the 1999 996 racer almost saw a repeat of the dominance of earlier years. Notable developments were the smaller diameter Öhlins forks and radial caliper Brembo brakes. *(Ian Falloon)*

Opposite: In his final full racing season Fogarty totally stamped his authority on the championship. *(Ian Falloon)*

More emphasis was placed on winning national Superbike championships, and in the US the 996 Factory machines were similar to the World Superbike racers but with 54mm throttle bodies as required by the AMA. They ran 46mm Öhlins forks and Dunlop tyres, and the increase in factory support was immediately evident in the results. Again there were two teams, Gobert and Bostrom on the Vance & Hines machines, and Matt Wait and Larry Pegram for Ferracci. Although Gobert won five races, neither he nor Bostrom were consistent enough to win the championship. But Ducati did win the manufacturers' title.

For the British and Australian championships there was the 996 Racing Special. Incorporating the MF3-S electronic injection system (with 60mm throttle bodies and three injectors), and the revised frame with larger airbox, the 996 RS was considerably higher in specification to the previous 996 Racing. The engine featured 39 and 32mm titanium valves, factory ported cylinder heads, shorter inlet tracts, and a 13mm lift inlet camshaft. Along with a sump extension in the crankcase the lubrication system was upgraded. With shorter Termignoni mufflers the 996 RS produced around 7–8bhp more than the 996 Racing of 1998. There were also upgraded specification four-pad Brembo brakes and 46mm Öhlins FG8750S forks and a DV7290 rear shock absorber. Only 11 996 RSs were produced for 1999. Troy Bayliss won the British Superbike Championship and Steve Martin the Australian Superbike Championship. There was a 996 Racing available for 1999, although only six were produced. These retained the twin injector Marelli P8 injection system.

2000

Expecting to continue Fogarty's dominance, Ducati Corse signed former AMA Superbike Champion Ben Bostrom in the official Team Ducati Infostrada. The 996 racer was still a formidable machine, but the team was very dependent on Fogarty and ill-prepared for his withdrawal from the championship. Finding a replacement proved more difficult than anticipated. After test rider Luca Cadalora failed, Troy Bayliss eventually assumed the role. Bostrom had difficulty adapting to the factory machine and its Michelin tyres, and was soon rel-

THE 916 AND BEYOND **149**

Fogarty in action in his final race, at Phillip Island 2000. *(Ian Falloon)*

By 2000 the 996 was at the peak of its development and about to make way for the Testastretta. *(Ian Falloon)*

egated to the satellite NCR team on Corser's 1999 racer. Juan Borja replaced Bostrom in the Infostrada line-up.

There were new cylinder heads (homologated through the 996 Factory Replica 2), with more material around the studs to improve stiffness and solve head gasket sealing problems. These heads also provided more material around the ports, leaving room for future development. The titanium valve sizes remained at 39mm inlet and 32mm exhaust, and the new camshafts provided less overlap. Computer simulation allowed for a complete reconfiguration of valve timing, compression ratio, porting, throttle body design, and injector position. This enabled an even higher compression ratio (over 13:1).

Another improvement was to the Marelli MF3-S injection system. While retaining 60mm throttle bodies there was now a single injector positioned above the throttle valve. Shorter or longer bell mouths altered the power requirements for individual tracks and there were 50–60mm (1.97–2.36in) shorter intakes, with the throttle bodies closer to the cylinder head. Because of the conical shape of the inlet tract these acted as if they were larger in diameter and flowed more. There were titanium Termignoni mufflers and 54mm exhausts. There was also more mid-range power. With 173bhp at a higher 12,000rpm, with the rev limiter set at 12,500rpm, the evolutionary process had yielded an increase of 15bhp over the previous three years.

The chassis and Pierobon frame was similar to the 1999 version, but there were revisions to the internal cartridge of the 42mm Öhlins forks, and different internal bleeding for the Öhlins shock absorber. The Marchesini wheels were still 3.50 x 17-inch on the front and either 6.00 x 17 or 16.5-inch on the rear. Previously the factory racers weighed slightly over the 162kg (357lb) minimum, but this year the weight was reduced near to the minimum. Pre-season testing also saw experimentation with a double-sided swingarm, with high exiting exhausts similar to the earlier 888. As these experiments proved inconclusive the distinctive single-sided swingarm was retained. There was also an updated Magneti Marelli data acquisition system, with more channels and memory increased to 24 MB (up from 2 MB).

It wasn't until the fifth round, at Monza, that Bayliss proved he was a front runner, but by this stage the championship was lost. Bayliss went on to win two races, Neil Hodgson two, and John Reynolds one. Ducati still won the constructors' championship but didn't have a rider in the top five. Apart from the official factory machines a further ten 996 Racing Specials were produced for selected teams in World Superbike and national championships. The specification included the revised single injector MF3-S Marelli injection system and a 57mm stainless steel exhaust system. These 162bhp machines were surprisingly close in performance to the official Team Ducati Infostrada racers. Both Hodgson, on the GSE entry, and Reynolds on the Red Bull machine were particularly impressive. Bayliss was originally signed alongside Steve Rapp in the Vance & Hines team for 2000 for the AMA Superbike Championship. With Ferracci losing his factory support Tim Pritchard's Ohio-based Competition Accessories team leased a 996 RS for Larry Pegram. When Bayliss moved to World Superbike Kocinski came in as a replacement but results were disappointing. In the British Superbike Championship Niall McKenzie joined Hodgson in the INS/GSE team, with James Haydon teaming with Reynolds on the Reve Red Bull 996 RS. The Ducatis dominated, Hodgson winning the championship.

2001

In an effort to regain their dominance, Ducati unleashed their first major engine development since the appearance of the Desmoquattro back in 1986. This was the second generation Desmoquattro, the Testastretta or 'narrow head'. The 15-year-old combustion chamber design was now limiting ultimate horsepower, as was the 66mm stroke. No longer the only twin cylinder racer, the Desmoquattro needed to be updated. During 1998 Massimo Bordi approached retired Formula One Ferrari engineer Ing. Angiolino Marchetti to assist in the design of the Testastretta. Marchetti worked closely with Bordi, but died during 1999 without seeing the project to fruition. Marchetti and Bordi decided on a 25° included valve angle, requiring a redesign of the Desmoquattro rocker layout. Marchetti's solution was to relocate the opening rocker arms outwards, keeping the closing rockers inside. To support the closing arms inside the head while maintaining a central spark plug, there was a central cast steel sleeve inserted for the

Being in the right place at the right time undoubtedly aided Bayliss in his promotion to the Infostrada Superbike team, but his results vindicated Ducati's decision. *(Ian Falloon)*

TROY BAYLISS

Although well known in Australia for his hard riding, it was a spectacular ride to sixth place on a woefully slow factory Suzuki RGV250 in the 1997 Australian 250cc Grand Prix that provided Troy Bayliss his big break. 'After the race Daryl Healey offered me a ride in his GSE team for the British Superbike series in 1998. It was a big move as I'd barely been outside Australia,' says Bayliss.

Troy Bayliss was born in the New South Wales country town of Taree, on 30 March 1969. Like any normal country boy on his parents' wheat farm, Bayliss began racing junior motocross and flat track, and was soon winning everything. Working as an automotive spray painter, at the age of 23 Bayliss took to road racing on a Kawasaki KR-1S production bike. His meteoric progress saw him on a Kawasaki ZX-6R in 1995, and second in the Australian Supersport Championship. He then graduated to a Team Kawasaki Australia Superbike in 1996, in which year he finished second in the Shell Superbike Championship and third in the Shell Oils Championship. For 1997 he earned a ride with Suzuki, taking the GSX-R750 to second place in both Australian Superbike Championships and two fifth places in the World Superbike race at Phillip Island. This resulted in his guest ride in the Australian GP that year.

Bayliss initially struggled in Britain. 'It was a tough first year. I had to learn the tracks and we had six DNFs due to mechanical failure. But the team wanted me back and winning the 1999 British Championship was a highlight for me.' An offer to compete in the AMA Superbike Championship saw the Bayliss family move to the US, where he immediately qualified on pole at Daytona. He didn't finish at Daytona, but went on to set pole position for the next race at Sears Point. Then Bayliss was called in as Fogarty's replacement at Sugo where he was run into in both races. 'It was a genuine racing incident and I felt like I was kicked in the teeth when Cadalora got the ride at Donington,' says Bayliss. But Ducati asked Bayliss to ride at Monza and when he gave them their first win of the season at Hockenheim his future was assured. At 32 years of age Bayliss had the maturity and tenacity to become Ducati's fifth World Superbike Champion.

For 2001 there was a new fairing, without side air scoops, to aid aerodynamics.
(Ian Falloon)

The heart of the 2001 racer was the new short-stroke Testastretta engine.
(Ian Falloon)

spark plug. The hollow camshafts also rotated in plain bearings, contributing to the more compact cylinder head. With a 100mm bore and 63.5mm stroke the new engine displaced 998cc, and provided room for larger 42mm and 34mm valves.

In line with racing engines since 1998 the sand-cast crankcases also featured a coppa bossa, or bottom cup, placing the oil pickup lower, although the crankcases were still not designed to accept a side-loading gearbox. Changing any internal ratios for racing still meant substituting an alternative engine. The cylinders were rotated backwards 10° to assist gravity oil scavenging from the front cylinder, and extensive use of titanium saw the racing engine weigh 66kg (146lb), 5kg (11lb) less than the production 996.

Inherited from the earlier 996 were the 60mm throttle body and MF3S Magneti Marelli electronic injection and ignition module with a single Marelli IWF1 injector per cylinder. Although the team tried a Marelli semi-automatic gearbox pre-season, testing was inconclusive and the gearbox was identical to the 2000 model 996. The more compact cylinder heads allowed for a larger capacity airbox and the exhausts were increased to 60mm. There was a larger and redesigned radiator and the 998 produced 174bhp at 12,000rpm, with a maximum of 12,500rpm. As the season progressed and the reliability of components was verified, the rev limit was increased to 13,000rpm.

The frame was made by Verlicchi this year, and there was revised Öhlins suspension. The 42mm front forks featured a sealed hydraulic cartridge, and a low friction spring as the fork was now pressurised. At the rear there was a larger reservoir. Brembo now supplied vented steel discs (290–305mm on the front and 218mm on the rear), providing reduced operating temperatures. The wheel sizes were standardised to 16.5-inch front and rear, with the rear rim width either a 6.00 or 6.25-inch. Homologated through the production 996 R was also a new fairing, without the upper side air scoops, and the machine was even closer to the minimum weight limit of 162kg.

Ducati Corse now supported two teams in World Superbike. In the Team Ducati Infostrada Bayliss was joined by the 23-year-old Spanish rider Ruben Xaus, who moved up from the World Supersport class. Ben Bostrom became a full works rider again, although

Troy Bayliss found the Testastretta 998 more to his liking, and his consistency gave him victory in the 2001 World Superbike Championship. *Ian Falloon)*

After winning the British Superbike Championship in 2000, Neil Hodgson made a full-time return to World Superbike on the GSE 996 RS during 2001. *(Ian Falloon)*

The year 2003 marks the return of Ducati to the Grand Prix arena for the first time since 1972. With this 990cc V-four they hope to emulate, and possibly eclipse, the success of the first 125cc desmo during the 1958 season.

with a separate L&M-sponsored team, on Dunlop tyres. Both teams were run under the direction of Tardozzi, and they were the only teams with the Testastretta engine for 2001.

Bayliss was immediately happier with the 998. 'It's faster, and suits me better than the old bike,' he said. His consistency soon saw him leading the championship and after a slow start Bostrom too began to win races. He won five races in succession and Xaus his first World Superbike victory at Oschersleben. This gave Ducati their tenth manufacturers' title and it was Bayliss, with six wins, who took out the riders' championship. At the final round at Imola Bayliss fronted with a silver paint scheme replicating the Imola 200 Formula 750 racers of nearly 30 years earlier. The dominance of the Testastretta in its inaugural season was not only a vindication of the excellence of the Testastretta design, but also the brilliance of Ducati's engineers.

The customer 996 RS retained the earlier 98 x 64mm 996cc engine. With the shorter intake system of the 2000 factory racers the power was increased to 168bhp at 12,000rpm. The forks were now 42mm Öhlins, with radial caliper Brembo front brakes, and the wheels were 16.5-inch front and rear. Although he didn't win any races, Hodgson proved surprisingly competitive against the new generation factory machines.

The 2001 season was one to forget in the US. Instead of factory machinery the two teams, HMC and Competition Accessories, operated 996 RSs. HMC signed former World Superbike Champion and five-times Daytona 200 winner Scott Russell on a one-year contract alongside Steve Rapp, but his season ended after a horrific start line accident at Daytona. Andreas Meklau later replaced Russell while Competition Accessories retained Larry Pegram, initially signing John Kocinski and later Aaron Slight, although neither ride eventuated.

To make up for the debacle in the US the Ducatis were even more dominant in Britain. On updated 996 RSs, the Reve Red Bull team of Reynolds and Emmett and the MonsterMob Ducati of Steve Hislop were unbeatable. The two veterans, Hislop and Reynolds, fought for the championship all year, Reynolds eventually prevailing after Hislop crashed out of the series at the penultimate round at Rockingham.

2002

There was no change to the official factory team line-up for 2002, but with the 998 always considered an interim model before the advent of the all-new 999 at the end of 2002, the factory racers received a second generation Testastretta engine. Now 999cc, with a 104mm bore and 58.8mm stroke, this coincided with a change in the minimum weight regulations. The 1,000cc twins' weight was now 164kg (362lb), with the 750cc fours 159kg (351lb), an intriguing reversal of the original regulations that were drafted when fours were dominant. This reflected the success of Ducati's process of continual evolution that again saw the Desmoquattro the leading Superbike.

In May 2001 Ducati Motor Holding announced their intention of developing a four-stroke GP 1 prototype to take advantage of new Grand Prix regulations. These allowed 990cc four-stroke prototypes to compete in the GP category, and marked Ducati's return to Grand Prix racing for the first time since the 500cc V-Twin of 1971 and 1972. With the design entrusted to Ducati Corse, initial indications were the GP 1 engine would be a radical desmodromic twin inserted in a tubular trestle frame. The aim was to build an innovative and competitive prototype that retained traditional features associated with Ducati. During February 2002 it was announced, after considering an oval piston twin cylinder engine, that further analysis led to a V-four with a simultaneous two-by-two firing order to maximise traction. The design team, headed by Filippo Preziosi, decided on a Desmosedici (Desmosixteen) capable of exceeding 18,000rpm.

Eventually Ducati will be involved with factory racing teams on two fronts: World Superbike to promote and develop the production range, and Grands Prix for the trialling of new technology. One thing is certain. Ducati can never be underestimated and although the situation in GP will be that of David and Goliath, the commitment and experience of Ducati Corse could see a new age of racing success.

INDEX

Index for photos in **Bold**

A

Albacete 124, 128, 136
Aberdare Park **32**
ACU 92
Adamo, Jimmy **95**, 105, 111
ADAC Eight Hour race 106
Adams, Jim **38**
Adelaide Three Hour race 92
Aermacchi 49, 67
Aero Caproni 12
Agostini, Giacomo 49, **51**, 54, **56**, 57, 64, 69, 100
Alessandria 28
Alfa Romeo 99
Alstare team 146
AMA 47, 71-72, 75, 148
AMA championships (races) 72, 75, 95, 124, 126, 128-129, **130**, 132, 142, 144, 148, 151-152
Amatriain, Daniel 126
America 44-45, 63, 71, **75**, 76
Andersson, Anders 140
Anelli, Luigi 64
Angel, Ron 64
Antoni, Gianni Degli 13-14, **16**, 18-19, 24, **26**, 28, 44
Aprilia 142
Arcarons, Jodi **111**
Argentina 45
Armaroli, Renato **36**, 45, **58**, 97, 113
Artusi 16, 24
Assen 28, **31**, 86, 104, 138, 147
Auriana, Larry 91
Auriol, Hubert 111
Australia **21**, 91-92, 94, 120, 138, 142, 152
Australian championships 130, 142, 148, 152
Austria 119
Austrian championships 141, 144
Autodromo Dino Ferrari 64

B

Baja 1000 49
Balboni, Amedco 44
Barcelona 39
Barcelona 24-hour race 18, 44-45, 49, **79**, **81**, 86, 105, 109, 111
Baracca, Francesco 14
Barchitta, Fabio 104
Baroncini, Sergio 57
Barone, Michel 44
Bass, Tony 'Slick' 138
Bartolozzi, Professor 114
Battle of the Twins 91, **95**, 105, 109, **110**, 111, 113, 117, 119, 124
Bayliss, Troy 145, 148, **152**, 154, **155**, 157
Belgium 81
Benelli 44, 50
Bergamo 21
Berliner 21, 34, 45, 49
Bilancione, Franco 132
Bilbao 35
Bimota **118**
Birmingham 36
Blackburn, Lancashire 138
Blora, Paolo 145
BMW 58, 64, 71-72, 75, **77**
Boinet 83
Bol d'Or 66, 71, 81-83, 111, 114, **115-116**, 140
Bol d'Or Italia 82, 105
Bologna 16, 34, 39, 44, 49, 59, 88, 135-136
Bologna Show 95, 99
Bologna Tangenziale 69
Bologna University 14, 114
Bordi, Massimo 114, 116-117, 131, 135-136, 151
Borgo Panigale 14, 44, 87, 97, 113
Borja, Juan 151
Boselli, Count 23
Bostrom, Ben 147-148, 151, 154, 157
Brainerd 122, 141
Branch, Jerry 72
Brands Hatch **31**, 34, 36, 49, 54, 64, 100, 147
Bratton, Jeff 72
Brazil 20
Brettoni, Augusto 51
Britain 88, 92, 152, 157
British Championships 31, **32**, 34, 100, 104, 140-141, 144, 148, 151-152, **157**
BRM 59
Brno 104
Broccoli, Massimo **98-99**, 120
Bryan, Ralph 49
BSA 64, 66, 88, 100
Bultaco 66, 81
Busi 114
Busto Arsizio **42**
Butenuth, Hans-Otto 64

C

Cadalora, Luca 148, 152
Cagiva 110-111, 113, 124, 132, 136, 138, 140
California 71, 75-76, 89
Camillieri, Frank 49
Camp, Vic 49, 51, 54, 63
Canada 44-45, 63-64, 71, 124
Canellas, Salvador **79-82**, 83, **86**
Caracchi, Rino 51, 87-88, 92, 126
Caracchi, Stefano 87, 111, 119
Caralt, Jaime 18
Cardus, Carlos 86, 111
Carini, Mario **17**
Caroli, Aldo 12
Carr, Cliff 64
Carruthers, Kel 71
Casoli, Paolo 141, **146-147**
Castiglioni brothers 113-114, 135
Castiglioni, Claudio 113
Castiglioni, Gianfranco 113
Castle Combe 38
Castrol Six Hour race 31 ,92
Cathcart, Alan 133
Catholic Church 13
Cavazzi, Piero 83, 87, 89, 94
Ceccato 14
Cervia 51
Cesenatico 34, 49, 51, 54
Chadwick, Dave **26**, 28
Chambon, Stéphane 140
Chili, Pier Francesco 140-142, 144
Ciceri, Santo **17**
Cobas, Antonio 110
Coburn and Hughes 71, 88, 91, 94
Coca Cola Eight Hour race 91
Cologne Show 99,132
Competition Accessories team 151, 157
Cooley, Wes 75
Cooper, John 64
Cooper, Vernon 92
Corfu 64
Cornwell, Jon 133
Corser, Troy **130**, 139-140, **141-142**, 144, 147, 151
Cosenza 50
Costa, Dott. Francesco 61
Cosworth 114
Cowie, John 92
Craig, Joe 14
Cromer, Leon 49
Cussigh, Walter 101, 104-106, 110
Cycle magazine 71, 76

D

Dahne, Helmut 64
Danna, Marcello 16
Daytona **44**, 45, 47, 49, 54, 61, 64, 66, 71-72, **73**, **75**, 76, **77**, 91, **95**, 105, 110-111, **117**,119, 126, 128, 133, 152, 157
DeEccher, Ing. 67, 79, 82
Del Piano, Guido 98
DEMM 17
De Petri, 'Ciro' 111
De Portago 18
Detroit 126
Dienza team 147
Domenicali, Claudio 131-132, 147
Donington 91-92, **118**, 119, 124-125, 128, 133, **137-138**, 139, 152
Doohan, Mick 142
Douglas, Dave 49
Drusiani, Alfonso 14
Ducati Corse 147-148, 154, 157
Ducati Motor Holding 157
Ducati Infostrada team **146**, 147-148, 151, **152**, 154
Ducati Performance team 144, 146-147
Dugdales 34
Dunrod 101
Dunscombe, Alan 54, **62**, 63-64

E

Earles, Ernie 36
Earls Court Motorcycle Show 59
Ecurie Sportive 31, **32**, 33-34, 49
EFIM 53
Elkhart Lake 141
Emde, Dave 64, 75
Emilia Romagna 14
Emmett, Sean 144-145, 157
England 20-21, 31, 34, 36, 49, 54, 59, 63-64, 66, 88, 92, 138
Estrosi, Christian 82-83
Europe 12, 54, 61, 95
European Championships 31, 99, 125, 133, 146, **147**
Everett, Reg 49
Eynsforsd, Kent 66

F

Facchini, Erino 43
Faenza 19
Falconi 16
Falappa, Giancarlo 122, **124**, 125-126, 128, 132, 136, **138**
Fantuzzi 16
Fargas, Ricardo 18, 44-45, 86
Farinelli, Aldo 12
Farnè, Alberto 12, 44
Farnè, Franco 12-13, **16-17**, 18, 21, 26, 28, 34-35, **36**, 39, **42**, **44**, 45, 47, 51, **55**, 61, **66**, 69, 87, 91, 98, 101, 105, 110
Fermo 16
Ferracci, Eraldo 87, 119, 126, 128-129, **130**, 139-140, 144-145, 148, 151
Ferrari cars 18, 59, 116, 144, 151
Ferrari, Enzo 14
Ferrari, Virginio 44, 81-82, **109**, 110, 116, 136, 138-142, 144
Ferri, Romolo **26**, **28**
Fiat 50
FIM 57
Findlay, Jack 64
Finmeccanica 97, 113
Fiorio, Giovanni 12
Fisherman's Bend 21
Florida 45
Fogarty, Carl 95, **124**, **126**, 128, **129**, **135**, 136, **137-138**, 139-140, **142-143**, 144-145, 147, **148**, **150**, 152
Fogarty, George 95, 138
Folesani, Oscar 31, 33, 36
Ford-Dunne, Martin 59
Foti, Serafino 144
Fort Wayne, Indiana 76
France 114, 124
Francini, Vanes 95, 98
Frasers 94
French Championships 44

G

Gallina, Roberto 49
Gandossi, Alberto 11-12, 18, 24, 26, 28, 50
Gardner, Wayne 91, 142
Garriga, Juan 109-111, 116, 128
Gattolone team 140-142
Geminiani 18
German championships 110, 128-130, 141, 145

Germany 64, 91, 130, 145
Gianesin, Pietro di 104, 128, 140, 147
Gilera 16, 26
Gio.Ca.Moto 146, **147**
Gitan 50
Giuliano, Ermanno 51, 54, **55**, **57**, 58, 61, 63-64, 83
Gobert, Anthony 145, 147-148
Godier-Genoud 81
Gramigni, Alessandro 141
Granada-Dakar rally **111**
Grands Prix
    Australian 152
    Belgium 28, **34**, 35-36
    Britain 138
    Canada 64
    Dutch **25**, **31**, 33-34
    Finland 21
    Germany 28, 33
    Greece 64
    Isle of Man (TT) **26**, **28**, 38
    Italy 37-38, 49, 57
    Nations 24, 26, 28, 33, 41, 50
    San Remo 49, **56**, 57
    South Africa (TT) 64
    Spain 39, 49
    Sweden 24, 28, 33
    Ulster 28, 33, 36
    US 45
    Yugoslavia 57
Gran Fondo road races 11, 18
Granie, Marc 106
Grant, Mick 69, 71
Grant, Ron 64
Grassetti, Silvio 64
Grau, Benjamin **79-82**, 83, **86**, 105, 109-111
Graziano, Antonio 13, **18**
GSE team 144-145, 151-152
Guareschi, Vittoriano 147
Guazzoni 17
Guichon, Philippe 106

H
Hailwood, Michelle 31
Hailwood, Mike 14, 20-21, 28, **31-32**, 33-35, **36**, 37, **38**, 49, **51**, 54, 58, **61**, 88-89, **90-91**, 92, **93**, 94-95
Hailwood, Stan 31, 33, 35-37
Hale, Mike 140, 145
Hanover 91

Hansen, Bob 66
Harley-Davidson 76
Harte, Keith 71
Hartle, John 36
Haydon, James 151
Healey, Daryl 152
Hedemora 24, 28
Helsinki 21
Herrero, Santiago 49
Hewland Gears 89
Higbee, Shawn 141
Hinton, Eric 21
Hislop, Steve 140, 144, 157
Hiyashi, Mr 91
HMC team 157
Hockenheim 33, 122, 128, 139, 152
Hocking, Gary 33
Hodgson, Neil 140, 142, 151, **157**
Holden, Robert 88, **133**
Holland 20
Honda 34, 36, 49, 64, 79, 82-83, 88, 92, 100, 111, 117, 124, **135**, 138, 142
Hutchinson 100 36, 64

I
Imola 14, 16, 34, 37, 49, **50**, 54, 57-58, 61, **62-64**, **66**, 67, **68**, 69, **70**, 71, 75-76, 79, **80**, 81, 87, 99, 105, **109**, 111, 157
Inzinger, Alfred 139
Igoa, Patrick 111
ISDT **12**
Isle of Man 21, 26, 28, **32**, 33-37, 51, 54, 71, 88, 91-92, **93**, 94-95, 99, **100**, 101, **104**, 105, 109-110, **133**, 138
Italian Championships 16, 18-19, 26, 28, 34, 41, **42**, 44, 49-51, 53, 58, 71, **94**, 95, **97-98**, 99, 101, **103**, 104-105, **109**, 110, 117, 119-120, 122, 124, 136, 141, 144-145, 147
Italian FMI regulations 13, 43
Italian Riviera street races 49
Italy 11-12, 18-19, 21, 31, 35-36, 39, 44-45, 49, 53, 57-59, 61, 104, 119, 145

J
James, Errol 64
James, Jamie 124

Japan **91**
Japanese Championships 126
Jarama 105
Jeffries, Tony 64
Jerez 105, 111, 122
John Player International 51, 58
Juan, Enrique de 86, 105, 110

K
Kavanagh, Ken **21**, 28, **32**, 33-34, **37**
Kawasaki 64, 66, 71-72, 75-76, 79, 92, 105, 128, 138, 152
Kipp, Tom 145
Kneubühler, Bruno **68**, 69, 71
Knight, Ray 82
Kocinski, John 140, **141**, 151, 157
Korhonen, Pentti 82
Kyalami 144, **145**

L
L&M team 157
Laconia 49
La Coruña, 35
La Ferla, Osca 105, **106**, 110
Laguna Seca **75**, 111, 140
Lambretta 17
Landi 12
Lansivuori, Tepi 71
LaPorte, Danny 111
Latvia 39
Laverda 12, 16, 51
Leandrini, Luciano 104
Leathemstown 28
Lega, Mario 86
Le Mans 81, **82**, 105, 124
Lenzi 114
Leoni, Reno **48**, 49, 87, 95, 110
Leopardi, Pierfrancesco 18
Lercaro, Cardinal 13
Librenti, Fuzzi 51, 54, **55-56**
Liège 24 Hours 106
Lindholm, Christer 141, 144
Lionello, Aurelia 114
Llewellyn, Matt 140
Loigo, Claudio 87
Lolli, Dott. Eugenio 16, 44
Longford 21
London 53
Loudon 95
Luc, Jacques 81
Lucchiari, Mauro 128, 133, 139-140

Lucchinelli, Marco 83, **109-110**, 111, **116-118**, 119, **120**, 122, 124
Lugo 14, 16
Lunn, Doug 71

M
Magee, Kevin 124
Maier, Hans 99
Maini, Ettore 12
Malaguti, Giovanni 12
Malibu Mountains 76
Mallol, Jose Maria 71, 82, 86
Mallory Park 36, 91-92, **93**
Manchester 88, 92
Mandolini, Giuseppe 18, 45
Mandracci, Guido 64
Manship, Steve 82, 88
Maoggi, Giuliano **11**, 13, 16, 18
Marchetti, Ing. Angiolino 151
Maranello 14
Maranghi, Mario 16, 18
Mark, Udo 130
Mariannini, Giovanni 83, **100**, 101
Marinoni, Giampaolo 111
Martin, Steve 148
Mastroela, Ugo 44
Mazzanti **55**, **68**
McClark, John 49
McGregor, Graeme 104-105
McKenzie, Niall 151
McLaughlin, Steve 72
Meklau, Andreas 129, 140-141, 144-145, 157
Menchini, Pietro 98
Mengoli, Gianluigi 98, 114, **115**, 116, 131
Mercedes-Benz 23
Merloni, Andrea 142
Mertens, Stéphane 126, 128
Mexico 51, 126
Mezzette 114
Michigan 126
Milan Show 71
Milano-Taranto 11, **12**, 16, 18, 50
Mille Miglia 18
Miller, Sammy 26, 28
Milvio, Arnaldo 53-54, 59
Misano 82-83, **85**, **90**, 92, 94, 99, 105, **106**, 111, 116, 119, **131**, 132
Mladin, Matthew 144
Modena 13, 17, 26, 34, 36, 39,

44, 47, 49-51, 54, **55**, **57**, 63, 69
Mondial 14, 17, 23-24, 26, 36, 44
MonsterMob team 157
Montano, Dott. Giuseppe 11, 13, 18, 21
Montanari, Alano 16, 18, **25**
Monti, Baldassare 119-120, 122
Montjuich Park 18, 44, 49, **80**, 81-83, **86**, 87, 100, 105, 110
Monza 12, 17, 24, 26, 28, 35, **37**, 38, 41, 44, 49-50, **56**, 57, 110, 119, 124, 140, 147, 151-152
Morbidelli 39
Morocco 111
Mortimer, Chas 51
Mosport 63-64, 124
MotoBi 16
Moto Cinelli 139
Motogiro d'Italia **11**, 12-13, **16**, **18**, **26**, **34**, 44,50
Moto Guzzi 17, 21, 26, 64
Mototrans 35, 39, 44-45
Mugello 81-82, 99, 106, 116, 138
MV Agusta 19, 24, 26, **28**, 33, 43, 50, 57, 59, 64, 69, 100
MZ 33, 45

N
Nardi and Danese 17, 24
Nation, Trevor 104
NCR 44, 69, 81-83, 86-89, 91, 94-95, 126, 151
Neilson, Cook 71-72, **73**, **75**, 76, **77**, 89
Nepoti, Giorgio 51, 69, 87, 126
Nepoti, Massimo 69
Neri, Renzo 92, 98
New South Wales 94, 142, 152
Newton, Dale 75
New York City 76
New Zealand 31, 92, 120
Nicholls, Roger 82, 88, 91-92, 94
Nieto, Angel
Norton 14, 21, 37, 64, 66, 88, 92, 100
NSU 21
Nürburgring 28, 86, 89, 106

O
Ohio 151
Ollioules 124

INDEX **159**

Ontario, California 66
Opatija 57
Orioli, Edi 111
Oschersleben 157
Österreichring 106, 122
Ostia 16
Oulton Park 34, 92

P

Paddock Wood 64
Pagani, Alberto 28, 57, 64
Palomo, Victor 83, 86
Paquay, Michael 146
Parilla 43
Paris-Dakar (Cape Town) rally 111
Parlotti, Gilberto 49, 51, 54, 57, 63-64
Pasolini, Renzo 49, 61
Paul Ricard 114
Pazzaglia, Sauro **94**, 95
Pedretti, Giuliano 88, 91, **100**, 101, 110
Pegram, Larry 141, 148, 151, 157
Pennati, Gaetano 12
Perugini, Carlo 82
Pesaro 57
Petrucci, Franco **12**
Pharaohs Rally, 111
Phillip Island **137**, **150**, 152
Phillis, Tom 34
Pickrell, Ray 64
Pininfarina 125
Pirovano, Fabrizio 139, 146
Polen, Doug 87, 124, **125-127**, 128-130
Portugal 101
Preziosi, Filippo 157
Pridmore, Reg 72
Princeton 76
Pritchard, Tim 151
Promotor 139-140, **141**, 142
Provini, Tarquino 26, 33
Purslow, Fron 20, 31, 34

Q

Quarterley, Dale 119

R

Race of Aces 64
Rainey, Wayne 117
Railton, Dave 95
Ramsay, Callum 133
Rapp, Steve 151, 157

Rayborn, Cal 71
Read, Phil 38, 49, 54, **56**, 57, 64, 88, 92, **93**
Recchia, Mario 12, 21, **25**, **36**, 37, **68**, **83**, 87
Rechtenbach, Dieter 110
Redman, Jim 21, 34, 36
Reiss, Wolfgang 91
Relats 18
Reve Red Bull team 144-145, 151, 157
Reyes, Luis 105, 109
Reynolds, John 144-145, 151, 157
Ricardo **59**,113
Ricci, Mauro 105
Riccione 49, 51
Rimini 49, 135
Rippa, Enzo 45
Ritter, Paul 75
Riva del Garda 18
Riverside 72
Rizzi, Rinaldo 87
Roche, Raymond 111, **120**, 122, **123-124**, 125-126, 128, 136
Rockett, George 45, 49
Rockingham 157
Roberts, Eddie 94
Roda 18
Roe, Dr 95
Rogers, Alistair 51
Rome 16
Russell, Scott 128, **129**, **138**, 139, 157
Rutter, Tony 64, 88, 95, 99, **100-104**, 105, 109-110
Rymer, Terry 138, 141

S

Saarinen, Jarno 61, 69, 71
Saccomandi, 12
Saltarelli, Carlo 71
San Petronius cathedral 16
Savelli, Aulo 39
Scamandri, Ettore 13, 16, 18
Scaysbrook, Jim 91-92, 94
Schanz, Bob 34
Schilling, Phil 71-72, **73**, 75-76, **77**, 89
Schlachter, Richard 95
Scuderia Due Torri 44
Scuderia Farnè-Stanazo 34
Scuderia Speedy Gonzales 51
Sear, John 88

Sears Point 75, 152
Sebring 45
Seeley, Colin 54, **55**, 66
Sestini, Marcello 18
Sheene, Barry 61, 63, 138
SIATA 12
Silverstone 36, **38**, 51, 54, 57-58, **61**, 71, 91-92
Simmonds, Dave 64
Simonetti, Rolando 124, 128
Skopia Locka 54
Slinn, Pat 88, 104
Slight, Aaron 157
Smart, Maggie 63, 66
Smart, Paul 49, 57-58, **62**, 63, **64**, **66**, **70**, 71
Smith, Bill 64
Snetterton 36, 54, 64
Sozzani, Salvatore 12
South Africa 64
Spa 33-36, 106
Spaggiari, Bruno 13, **16**, 18, 21, 26, 28, 33, 35, 39, 44-45, 49, **50-51**, 54, **55**, 57-58, 61, **62-63**, 64, **66**, **68**, 69, **70**, 71
Spain 34-35, 44-45, 49, 79, 105
Spanish Championships 71, 86
Spairani, Fredmano 53-54, **55**, 59, 61, 63-64, 66-67
Spencer, Freddie 95, 140
Sports Motorcycles 82, 88, 91-92, 95, 99-100, 104, 138
Sprayson, Ken 36, 38
Stevens, Thomas 144-145
Sugo 124, 142, 152
Surtees, John 36-38
Surtees, Norman 36
Suzuki 31, 66, 95, 99, 105, 126, 152
Suzzi, Filippo 105
Symmonds Plains 21
Sweden 20, 24
Switzerland 20, 45

T

Taglioni, Biagio 14
Taglioni, Fabio **11**, 12-13, **14-15**, 16-17, 19, 21, **23**, 24, **26**, 28, 33-35, 37-39, 44, 49, 53-54, 57-59, 61, 63-64, **66**, 67, **68**, 69, 71, 79, 81-82, 87-88, 95, 97-98, 105, 110-111, 113-114, 116, 131
Tait, Percy 34, 63-64

Tamarozzi, Ugo 11, **12**
Tamburini, Massimo 135-136
Tamworth-in-Arden 31
Tardozzi, Davide **118**, 120, 125-126, 128, 132, 136, 139, 144, 147, 157
Taree 152
Tartarini, Leopoldo 13, **16**, **34**
Tasmania 21
Taveri, Luigi 26, 28, **31**, 33, **34**
Team Grottini 128
Team Hansen 63
Tecfar 110-111
Tecno 58
Tejedo, Alejandro 82, 86
Temporada di Primavera 49
Terblanche, Pierre 128, **131-132**
Texas 126
Texas Pacific Group 142
Thomas, Dean 147
Thruxton 81-82
Tonkin, Steve 88
Toschi, Danilo 124
Trento 12
Triumph 63-64, 66, 88
Tumidei, Ing. Bruno 59
Tunisia Rally 111
Turku 21
Turin 12

U

Ubbiali, Carlo 19, 24, 26, **28**, 50
Ulster 101, 104
UK 43, 95, 144-145
Uncini, Franco 50, 71, 126
US 34, 43, 44-45, 49, 71, **91**, 95, 126, 130, 140-141, 144-145, 148, 152, 157

V

Valladolid 35
Vallelunga 105
Valli Bergamasche **12**
Vance & Hines 144-145, 148, 151
Varese 113, 132
Venezuela 20
Venzano Casina 50
Vial, Alain 81
Victoria (Australia) 64
Vila Real 101, 104-105, 110
Villa, Francesco 13, 16, 18-21, 26, 28, 33-34, 41, 44, 82
Villa, Walter 64, 71, 82, **106**
Vincenzi, George 95

VM Group 97, 113
Vuillemin, Didier 106

W

Wait, Matt 148
Wales 12
Webster, Marvin 72
Weibel, Edwin 128-129
Westlake Village 76
Wheeler, Arthur 34
White, Richard 64
Whitham, James 139
Williams, John 49, 64
Williams, Ron 95, 101
Woollongong 142
World Championships (races)
    Coupe d'Endurance 58, 81-82, 86, 88, 95, 100
    Endurance 105-106, 110, 124, 126, 138
    Formula 1 (TT1) 88, **91**, 92, **93**, 94-95, 100, 105, 109-111, 138
    Formula 2 (TT2) 98-99, **100**, 101, 104-105
    Formula 750 57-58, 64
    Grand Prix 124, 126, 157
    Superbike 71, **118**, 119-120, 122, **123**, 124, **125-127**, 128, 133, 135, **137-8**, 139-47,151-152, 154, **155**, **157**
    Supersport **146-147**, 154
World War One 14
World War Two 12, 14
Wynne, Steve 82, 88-89, **90**, 91-92, 94-95, 99, 101, 124

X

Xaus, Ruben 147, 154

Y

Yamaha 47, 49, 61, 66, 69, 76, 99-100, 124
Yoshimura, Fujio 72
Yoshimura, Pops 72
Yugoslavia 54

Z

Zauibouri, Franco 82
Zaragoza 34
Zeltweg 119, 129
Zitelli, Glauco **12**